CONFIRMATION

*Anointed and Sealed
with the Spirit*

Rituals and Retreats

Rituals by Robert W. Piercy
Retreats by Jean E. Bross

Living the Good News, Inc.
a division of The Morehouse Group
Denver, CO

We dedicate this book to Melissa Cuddy, whose spirit has empowered us to share our gifts. Happy confirmation!

—Bob and Jean

Imprimatur pending.

Project Coordinator: Robert W. Piercy
Project Editors: Dirk deVries and Kathy Coffey
Cover Design: Val Price
© 1997 by Robert W. Piercy and Jean E. Bross

All music referred to in the rituals is available in recorded form. Contact these publishers for more information:

GIA Publications
7404 S. Mason Ave., Chicago, IL 60638
Order Line: 1.800.422.1358
FAX: 1.708.496.3828
E-mail at custser@giamusic.com

Oregon Catholic Press (OCP)
5536 N.E. Hassalo, Portland, OR 97213
Order Line: 1.800.LITURGY (548-8749)
FAX: 1.800.4-OCP.FAX (462-7329)
E-mail at liturgy@ocp.org

Living the Good News, Inc.
a division of The Morehouse Group
Editorial Offices
600 Grant Street, Suite 400
Denver, CO 80203

Printed in the United States of America.

ISBN 1-889108-32-4

Table of Contents

PART ONE: Rituals for Confirmation

Introduction to the Rituals

The Basic Principles of Ritual

Rituals for confirmation was written with the idea that many possible adaptations are needed since no two parishes are alike. Although this is a catechetical program, it is steeped in ritual and liturgy. The premise of the rituals is based on five basic principles of ritual:

- community
- repetition
- symbols
- awe and wonder
- affirmation and challenge

Community

We do not pray alone. Instead we gather as a group of people. This means we bless the candidates within a community liturgy and the individual rituals happen with more than just candidates present. It would be ideal if the entire parish, or at least members of the community, were invited to participate for any ritual in this book.

Repetition

The art of any good ritual is repetition, so that the assembly is not surprised. Instead, those present feel comfortable with the "flow of things"—enough so that they feel free to enter into the mystery of the prayer, find their inner selves and share themselves with the community. Often we feel uncomfortable with repetition because we fear it may become boring. It becomes boring if those who lead the prayer make it that way. Take for instance, "The Lord be with you!"—this phrase, although repeated often in the rituals, is charged with emotion; how we say it changes each time because we are different each moment in life. Our wish and desire to have the Lord be with someone changes with our rhythm of life.

Symbols

We need to stop explaining and controlling symbols. Let them speak for themselves. Allow them to lead our spirituality. As leaders of prayer, as members of assembly we simply bring the symbols of earth, air, fire and water to the worshiping assembly and then allow the assembly movement within these symbols.

Awe and Wonder

The beauty of ritual is that there is a natural awe and wonder to prayer. So often we try to manufacture feelings around prayer. Prayer comes from our center and the belief that we are praising God. From there we find our need and desire to pray. Prayer is not magic, it simply has an awe and wonder that calls us beyond the age of computers. Ritual is not binary, it can be so many things. Ritual allows us to open hearts and minds to those many possibilities.

Affirmation and Challenge

The final step of any ritual is an affirmation of the assembly and a challenge to move. The words "Go, in the peace of Christ" is more than a nice ritual piece of language. It needs to be packed with the energy of support and the movement to go on. So often ritual is looked upon as another event that got us to an end instead of moving us to the end of a page which begs to be turned for the next phrase.

Basic Premises of the Rituals

Ministries

Who is the primary minister? *The assembly.* So often we forget that and try to find other "things" for the assembly to do. Their presence and participation is the greatest gift they bring. All other ministries flow from and to the assembly. Other ministers are servants of the assembly.

Presider

The presider (leader of prayer) would ideally be a lay person of the community. Although this could be an ordained presbyter, it does not have to be. It should, however, be a leader. To simply move the role from person to person because you may want everyone to "have a chance" defeats the purpose of this ministry. This should be a person comfortable in front of a large group, easy with gesture and able to communicate the awe and wonder of the prayer. Feel free to seek members of the community who have these qualities and ask them to help with the rituals if they cannot help with the entire program.

Readers

Again choose from the ability to minister the task, not from the need to give everyone an opportunity to do something. Readings are taken from the lectionary (rite of confirmation). Read from a lectionary or Bible, but not from a paper. The text of the readings are purposely not written here since it is the writer's belief that we should always prepare a ritual with a bible or lectionary near by. Mark your readings and have them ready for the reader to rehearse. Since many of the passages are short make sure the reader knows the meaning of what he/she may be reading since they will have to convey this message within a few short lines. Again, look at those who already minister as readers in the community. If not part of the Confirmation program, these readers may be willing to help in this period.

Musicians

Music is integral to each ritual. Not to sing would be like saying the words "Happy Birthday" and not singing them. The impact of the birthday would lose so much. Music that was suggested was always thought of in the broadest sense of parish repertoire. Although specific suggestions were given, general topics were also suggested. In choosing music make sure it is singable by all present. During the rituals you may want to introduce music that may be used as part of the actual Confirmation. Although an instrumentalist, a percussionist and a leader of song would be ideal, you can simply do each ritual with a leader of song. This ministry calls for someone who can animate an assembly and call a community into song. Again, look at your own ministers of music and let them know about these rituals. The relationship of the music ministry and the confirmation candidates can happen early in the formation process.

Sacristan

Although not actually needed to be present at each ritual, the sacristan makes sure that each ritual has the items needed. Each of the rituals in this book begins with a checklist of needed materials; add other items as you wish. Just remember to give a sacristan time to prepare. Please don't turn ritual preparation into a last-minute scavenger hunt! Remember to ask this person to either take care of vessels and putting back things after an event, or find out where things should be placed for clean-up at a later time.

A Closer Look at the Rituals

For each unit, we provide more than enough prayer texts. The amount of prayers was based on the concept that for each unit there would be two catechetical sessions. If this is not the case for your setting choose from each unit the rituals you would use.

The blessing of candidates is to happen within the eucharistic assembly at the end of the liturgy. Before the final dismissal it is appropriate to bless many different groups. This could be one of the blessings.

In some settings the candidates and catechists may head directly to a catechetical session, but that is not necessary. Even if a session is scheduled sometime during the week, this blessing is still appropriate. The intent is to involve the community in praying for all those involved. The sign value is that the community sees itself as the mentors of the candidates and prays with them during their time of preparation.

The prayer to begin the catechetical session is much like the blessing. Don't hesitate to do both; again, repetition would not hurt and perhaps the repeating of the words would be helpful to all involved.

The extended rituals are intended for the end of the session. It would be wonderful to have members of the community present. If not, at least have catechists and invite parents, families and sponsors to be present. Each ritual takes about twenty minutes. By inviting the families and sponsors you are creating the community that will most likely be present for the sacrament itself, thus giving everyone a chance to get to know one another prior to the confirmation day itself.

As mentioned above, a checklist is provided. Use it as a guide and add your own needs.

Gathering

Gatherings are done in a variety of ways, usually with music. There is no procession unless directed. Therefore, the presider and other ministers are already in place. Environment is important. Find a place that suits the number of people present. Make sure vessels and other things used can be seen and are of a quality dignified for the assembly. Don't let anything be an afterthought. Contact those involved in parish art and environment and ask for their help. Getting them involved from beginning will help in the preparation of the sacrament.

An opening prayer should be proclaimed with an orans gesture. This is the uplifting of the hands with palms up to the heavens. Do not hold the book with one hand and lift the other. Use both arms and have an assistant hold the book.

Scripture

Scripture is presented in two formats:

- When reading from the Old Testament or the Acts of the Apostles, use someone other than the presider (leader of prayer). The community remains seated for this reading.
- When a gospel is proclaimed, let this be done by the presider (leader of prayer), since in our Sunday celebration of eucharist this is how it is done. The reading of a gospel begins with the singing of an acclamation. This would be an alleluia, except during Lent, when we don't say or sing alleluia—instead use a line of praise, e.g., "Praise to you Lord Jesus Christ, King of endless glory." If for some reason there is no music do not say the words or say alleluia, simply omit this section. During the singing of the gospel acclamation the assembly would stand. A procession with incense, candles and lectionary (or bible) would be very appropriate When proclaiming the gospel remember to use the full format of...

> *Presider*: The Lord be with you.
> *Assembly*: And also with you.
> *Presider*: A reading from the holy gospel according to N.,
> *Assembly*: Glory to you, Lord.

After the gospel:

> *Presider*: The gospel of the Lord.
> *Assembly*: Praise to you, Lord Jesus Christ.

The posture for the gospel is to be standing from the sung acclamation through the final line of "Praise to you, Lord Jesus Christ."

Silence and Reflection

After the readings a silence is suggested or a short reflection. A reflection would be wonderful and should be based upon the scripture in light of the catechetical session. For further ideas, look at the Adult Reflection for each unit in *Confirmation: Anointed and Sealed with the Spirit Leader's Guide*. If doing a reflection, the presider should be knowledgeable of the document "Fulfilled in Your Hearing" published by the Bishops of the United States. This document offers insight into the ministry of preaching that can greatly help lay people do scripture reflection.

Ritual Actions

Ritual actions need to be carefully thought through. Because each is unique, each community needs to adapt them to its specific needs. Know that each ritual had been done in some format with communities of varying sizes; they do work! For these rituals, the presider will need to go over the action in a rehearsal setting in the space. This should be a simple rehearsal where any ministers involved would go over things like where they will stand, where bowls or water will be place, where bread may be shared. This rehearsal is for the presider to become comfortable enough with the words and actions so that he/ she may be free from the book so as to communicate the idea to the assembly. A note here about the laying of hands: It was not specified where on the body the placing of hands would happen. It is suggested that those taking part feel comfortable with the gesture. Depending on the age group the head might be appropriate. Otherwise you may lay hands on shoulders or extended hands. Again, realize that this gesture of touch is to be done in silence. It is the blessing gesture and the silent prayer that is the central action. Modeling done by presider and one other person at the beginning of a ritual action would be appropriate. Any blessings, laying of hands or processions should be done with dignity and great gesture so that the assembly can fully enter the prayer.

The rituals end with the same format: the Lord's Prayer and a blessing. Again, gestures are important here. Use the orans gesture for the Lord's Prayer and the Sign of the Cross for blessing.

The concluding music usually repeats the opening song. This is offered as a suggestion. Often a repeat of the opening makes it simpler for the music ministry and the assembly. But, sending forth could be done in silence, or with a simple instrumental piece of music or another song that would fit the setting.

Special Notes

Unit 4, Ritual A includes an extended Penitential Rite. We suggest that candidates attend a parish reconciliation service instead of participating in this rite. Even if the candidates have not made their first reconciliation they should still attend the service and experience the community asking for forgiveness. If candidates are able to take part fully in the sacrament it would be appropriate for the catechist to do some simple examination of conscience prior to attending the service so as to help candidates prepare themselves to fully take part in the sacrament. Breaking open the experience after the sacrament would also support the learning process.

"Preparing for the Rite: An Overview" (p. 60) is not to be used as a teaching tool but as an experience for those who will minister in the sacrament or an evening for parents and sponsors. Every diocese has its own specifications. This commentary was written with full respect of that concept. Hopefully the commentary will serve simply as a reflection and guide through the rite itself.

If anything, look at this book, not as a book of experiences engraved in stone, but as a set of possible ways of celebrating the journey to and from the sacrament of confirmation. It is a journey of the entire worshiping community.

Rituals for Unit

1

Ritual A: Water Ritual

Note: This ritual, used initially in Unit 1, will be repeated in Unit 5. When used in Unit 5, replace the word *candidates* with the words *newly confirmed.*

Blessing of Candidates

(if used within the context of a eucharistic assembly)

Presider:
I invite the candidates for confirmation to come forward.

(After the candidates have come forward, the presider continues:)
Bow your heads and ask for God's blessing.

(Presider extends hands in blessing over candidates; you may wish to invite others in the assembly to extend their hands as well.)

Presider:
God of light and life.
Your Holy Spirit led Peter
to share your message throughout the land.
He was anointed with the Holy Spirit by your power.
Bless these candidates
as they continue on their journey toward confirmation.
Bless these catechists
as they proclaim of the power of Christ Jesus in their lives.
Bless this assembly
as we try to live as witnesses of the gospel to our candidates.
May our lives be enriched by this journey.
May we be blessed, Father, Son and Holy Spirit.

Assembly:
   Amen.

Opening Session
(if done at the beginning of the catechetical session)

Presider:
   God of light and life.
   Your Holy Spirit led Peter
   to share your message throughout the land.
   He was anointed with the Holy Spirit by your power.
   Be with these candidates
   as they continue on their journey toward confirmation.
   Be with these catechists
   as they proclaim of the power of Christ Jesus in their lives.
   May our lives be enriched by this journey.
   May we be blessed, Father, Son and Holy Spirit.

Assembly:
   Amen.

● ●

Ritual
Materials
   Bible
   lit candle
   pitcher of water
   large bowl

Gathering
(As the community gathers, create an assembly of sounds, for example, ran-
dom ringing of handbells, wind chimes, water sticks, etc. Combine sounds
that encourage the imagination and free the spirit. Over these sounds the
cantor begins to intone the refrain of "Song Over the Waters" by Marty

Haugen, GIA Publications, Inc., "We Shall Draw Water" by Paul Inwood, OCP Publications, or another refrain featuring water imagery. As the assembly repeats the refrain, bring forward a pitcher of water in procession.)

Presider:
In the name of the Father, Son and Holy Spirit.

Assembly:
Amen.

Presider:
The Lord be with you.

Assembly:
And also with you.

Presider:
We gather this day
to remember the outpouring of love and grace
that comes from the Holy Spirit.
This brings about the transformation of those
who accept and believe.
Let us pray:

(Presider pours water into bowl, lifting the pitcher high so that we hear the sound of water. The generous splashing of water is appropriate.)

God,
your spirit moved upon the waters of the Red Sea,
allowing the Israelites to move
from bondage to freedom.

(Sing one invocation of the gathering refrain.)

God,
your spirit moved upon the waters
that baptized Christ in the river Jordan,
showing all the people your great love.

(Sing one invocation of the gathering refrain.)

God,
your spirit moves upon your people
each time we gather for the sacrament of baptism,
witnessing the dying and rising of new life.

(Sing one invocation of the gathering refrain.)

Praise you, God,
for the gift of this water,
the gift of the Spirit
and the power of transformation they call forth from us.

(Sing one invocation of the gathering, then observe a period of silence.)

Scripture: John 7:37-39

(Presider invites the assembly to stand and sing an acclamation.)

Presider:
The Lord be with you.

Assembly:
And also with you.

Presider:
A reading from the holy Gospel according to John.

Assembly:
Glory to you, Lord.

(Presider reads John 7:37-39. After the reading is ended, presider continues:)

Presider:
The gospel of the Lord.

Assembly:
Praise to you, Lord Jesus Christ.

(Presider invites the assembly to be seated. The assembly observes a period of silence or hears a short reflection on scripture.)

Ritual Action

Presider:

I invite each candidate to come forward with their sponsor, parent
or catechist and to be blessed with these waters of new life.

*(As each candidate come forward, sponsor lays hands on candidate in silent
prayer. Sponsor then dips cupped hand in water and pours water over head
of candidate saying: "N., may you be blessed in the name of the Father, Son
and Holy Spirit. Amen." Candidate then returns to his or her seat. If there
are many candidates, divide water from the large bowl into several smaller
bowls and set up several stations for the ritual. Provide background music
or sounds, perhaps using the music and instruments used during the
gathering.)*

(Presider invites assembly to stand.)

Presider:

Let us pray in the words Christ has given us:

Assembly:

Our Father...
For the kingdom and the power and the glory are yours,
now and forever.
Amen.

Presider:

The Lord be with you.

Assembly:

And also with you.

Presider:

May almighty God bless us all, Father, Son+ and Holy Spirit.

Assembly:

Amen.

Presider:

Let us go forth and bear witness to the word of God.

Assembly:
Thanks be to God.

(Conclude by singing the final verse and refrain of the gathering song.)

• •

Alternative Closing Prayer
(if not presenting the ritual)

Presider:
God,
your spirit moved upon the waters of the Red Sea,
allowing the Israelites to move
from bondage to freedom.
Your spirit moved upon the waters
that baptized Christ in the river Jordan,
showing all the people your great love.
Your spirit moves upon your people
each time we gather for the sacrament of baptism,
witnessing the dying and rising of new life.
Praise you, God,
for the gift of water,
the gift of the Spirit,
and the power of transformation they call forth from us.

Assembly:
Amen.

Ritual B: Table-Setting Ritual

Blessing of Candidates

(if done within the context of a eucharistic assembly)

Presider:
    I invite the candidates for confirmation to come forward.

(After the candidates have come forward, the presider continues:)
    Bow your heads and ask for God's blessing.

(Presider extends hands in blessing over candidates; you may wish to invite others in the assembly to extend their hands as well.)

Presider:
    Faithful and loving God,
    You gave us your Son
    to show us the ways of truth.
    Bless these candidates
    as they gather to give you thanks and praise
    on their journey toward the sacrament of confirmation.
    Bless their catechists
    who are called to remember and celebrate their faith
    with these your children.
    Bless this community
    that spiritually journeys with our candidates.
    May we always remember, celebrate and praise you
    for the many gifts you give us.
    We are all blessed, Father, Son and Holy Spirit.

Assembly:
    Amen!

Opening of Session

(if done at the beginning of the catechetical session)

Presider:
    Faithful and loving God,
    You gave us your Son
    to show us the ways of truth.

Be with these candidates
as they gather to give you thanks and praise
on their journey toward the sacrament of confirmation.
Be with their catechists
who are called to remember and celebrate their faith
with these your children.
May we always remember, celebrate and praise you
for the many gifts you give us.
We are all blessed, Father, Son and Holy Spirit.

Assembly:
    Amen.

● ●

Ritual

Materials

Bible
table
table setting familiar to your community (examples: tablecloth,
    dishes, silverware, candles, flowers, etc.)
fresh loaf of bread

Gathering

*(As the assembly gathers around the table and instrumental music plays —
for example, "Come to Your Feast" by Michael Joncas, GIA Publications, or
"Gather Us Together" by Owen Alstott, OCP Publications — volunteers set
the table as if preparing for a dinner of family and friends. When the table
has been set, the music continues as presider speaks:)*

Presider:
    In the Name of the Father, Son and Holy Spirit.

Assembly:
    Amen.

Presider:
The Lord be with you.

Assembly:
And also with you.

Presider:
We gather today
not only to remember our baptism into the community,
but also our call to share with the community.
This table,
like so many of our home tables,
calls us to do more than just dine;
we are called to sacrifice.
We are called to give thanks,
to break and to share.
Let us sing together:

(Sing refrain of the gathering song.)

Presider:
Let us pray:
God of unconditional love,
You have called us all to the table.
The greatest and the least are welcome—
as are our stories.
May we take the time to remember
and to give thanks and praise.
We know all things come from you
who are God for ever and ever.

Assembly:
Amen.

Scripture: Luke 10:21-24

(Presider invites the assembly to sing an acclamation.)

Presider:
The Lord be with you.

Assembly:
   And also with you.

Presider:
   A reading from the holy Gospel according to Luke.

Assembly:
   Glory to you, Lord.

(Presider reads Luke 10:21-24. After the reading, presider continues:)

Presider:
   The gospel of the Lord.

Assembly:
   Praise to you, Lord Jesus Christ.

(Presider invites the assembly to be seated. The assembly observes a period of silence or hears a short reflection on scripture.)

Ritual Action

(Presider moves to table and begins to break the bread.)

Presider:
   Every time we gather at table
   we are asked not only to break bread
   but to share our stories—
   stories of people's lives who have formed us,
   stories of our own lives.
   Let us take a moment to reflect on someone
   who has showed us faith.
   As I pass this bread around
   I ask you to tell us about that person
   and to end your telling by saying:
   "I thank you God for the gift of N.,"
   naming the person once again.

(Presider begins by breaking off a piece of bread and sharing a story, then passes the bread to another member of the assembly. You might consider breaking the assembly into smaller groups of 5-7 members each; presider

then gives each group a piece of the original loaf. Encourage groups to link the action of the breaking of the bread with the telling of each story. To conclude, presider invites everyone to eat of the bread.)

Presider:
Let us now stand
and as one family
pray in the words Christ has given us:
Our Father...
For the kingdom, the power and the glory are yours now and forever.

Assembly:
Amen.

Presider:
The Lord be with you.

Assembly:
And also with you.

Presider:
As we go forth from this space
may we be blessed,
Father, Son and Holy Spirit.

Assembly:
Amen.

Presider:
Let us go forth in the peace of Christ.

Assembly:
Thanks be to God.

(Conclude by singing together the song used in today's gathering, or another eucharistic song.)

Alternative Closing Prayer

(if not presenting the ritual)

Presider:
> God of unconditional love,
> you have called us all to the table.
> The greatest and the least are welcome—
> as are our stories.
> May we take the time to remember
> and to give thanks and praise.
> We know all things come from you
> who is God for ever and ever.

Assembly:
> Amen.

Rituals for Unit

2

Ritual A: Presentation of Bibles and Laying on of Hands

Blessing of Candidates

(if used within the context of a eucharistic assembly)

Presider:
    I invite the candidates for confirmation to come forward.

(After the candidates have come forward, the presider continues:)
    Bow your heads and ask for God's blessing.

(Presider extends hands in blessing over candidates; you may wish to invite others in the assembly to extend their hands as well.)
    God of justice and truth,
    You have called us
    to be ministers to all on earth.
    Bless these candidates
    as they go forth to learn of your faithfulness.
    Bless their catechists
    as they share the wonders of your glad tidings.
    Bless this community
    as we continue our journey with these candidates.
    May we all recognize how blessed we are by your love.
    May we be blessed, Father, Son and Holy Spirit.

Assembly:
    Amen.

Opening Session

(if done at the beginning of the catechetical session)

Presider:
> God of justice and truth,
> You have called us
> to be ministers to all on earth.
> Be with these candidates
> as they go forth to learn of your faithfulness.
> Be with their catechists
> as they share the wonders of your glad tidings.
> May we all recognize how blessed we are by your love.
> May we be blessed, Father, Son and Holy Spirit.

Assembly:
> Amen.

• •

Ritual
Materials
Bible
lit candles
incense
gift Bibles, 1 per candidate

Gathering

(While the Bible is enthroned, sing an extended alleluia with verses, for example, "Halle, Halle" by Bell, Maule and Haugen, GIA Publications, or "Celtic Alleluia" by Christopher Walker and Fintan O'Carrol, OCP Publications. Use candles and incense.)

Presider:
> In the name of the Father, Son and Holy Spirit.

Assembly:
Amen.

Presider:
The Lord be with you.

Assembly:
And also with you.

Presider:
As we end this session,
we are called to open our hearts and minds
to the words of God present in scripture.
Let us pray:
God of comfort,
Your words call us to serve the world
with justice and righteousness.
Open our hearts and minds
to all the scripture can offer.
Make us instruments of your goodness.
We praise you as the God who lives forever and ever.

Assembly:
Amen.

Presider:
Let us be seated for the reading of the scripture.

Scripture: Isaiah 11:1-4

(Presider reads Isaiah 11;1-4. After the reading, there may be silence or a short reflection on scripture.)

Psalm 19

(The assembly sings together a setting of Psalm 19.)

(The assembly observes a period of silence.)

Ritual Action

(Presider invites the assembly to stand.)

Presider:
  Let us pray:
  God of gladness,
  Your words are everlasting life.
  Bless us as we continue to break open your word.
  May our journey always be grounded
  in the truths found in your scripture.
  We pray this through Christ our Lord.

Assembly:
  Amen.

(Presider presents each candidate with a Bible — one candidate at a time — saying to the candidate:)

Presider:
  N., receive the Word of God.
  May you find within these pages
  words of truth and comfort.

(Presider then silently lays hands on the candidate before presenting the next Bible. Both candidates and catechists may join in this rite as well. If there are many candidates, catechists could also present the Bibles. Candidates can have hands laid on them by several catechists and/or candidates. Remember, the laying on of hands is always done in silence.)

Presider:
  Let us now join in the words Christ himself has given us:

Assembly:
  Our Father...
  For the kingdom and the power and the glory are yours,
  now and forever.
  Amen.

Presider:
  The Lord be with you.

Assembly:
  And also with you.

Presider:
May almighty God bless us all, Father, Son+ and Holy Spirit.

Assembly:
Amen.

Presider:
Let us go forth to live the words of scripture.

Assembly:
Thanks be to God.

(Conclude by singing together the song used in today's gathering.)

• •

Alternative Closing Prayer
(if not presenting the ritual)

Presider:
God of comfort,
Your words call us to serve the world
with justice and righteousness.
Open our hearts and minds
to all the scripture can offer.
Make us instruments of your goodness.
We praise you as the God who lives forever and ever.

Assembly:
Amen.

Ritual B: Candle-Lighting Ritual and Renewal of Baptismal Promises

Blessing of Candidates

(if done within the context of a eucharistic assembly)

Presider:
  I invite the candidates for confirmation to come forward.

(After the candidates have come forward, the presider continues:)

Bow your heads and ask for God's blessing.

(Presider extends hands in blessing over candidates; you may wish to invite others in the assembly to extend their hands as well.)

Presider:
  God of love,
  You have given us the Spirit of truth.
  Bless these candidates
  as they go forth to learn of your unconditional love,
  Bless their catechists
  as they share the truth of your Spirit.
  Bless this community
  as we continue our journey with these candidates.
  May we always faithfully keep your commandments.
  And may we be blessed, Father, Son and Holy Spirit.

Assembly:
  Amen.

Opening of Session

(if done at the beginning of the catechetical session)

Presider:
  God of love,
  You have given us the Spirit of truth.
  Be with these candidates
  as they go forth to learn of your unconditional love.

Be with their catechists
as they share the truth of your Spirit.
May we always faithfully keep your commandments.
And may we be blessed, Father, Son and Holy Spirit.

Assembly:
Amen.

• •

Ritual
Materials
Bible
large, lit paschal candle
tapers, 1 per person (candidates and adults), to be distributed before
    the start of the ritual
incense

Gathering
(Percussive beat begins. Cantor intones "Lumen Christe" from Come All Ye
People: Shorter Songs for Worship, *John Bell, ed., GIA Publications, or
"Light of Christ" by Marty Haugen, GIA Publications. Lead procession with
incense, followed by paschal candle and Bible.)*

Presider:
In the name of the Father, Son and Holy Spirit.

Assembly:
Amen.

Presider:
The Lord be with you.

Assembly:
And also with you.

Presider:
  This day (night) we gather in glow of the Easter light,
  the candle of our baptism.
  On this journey
  we renew the promises made at baptism.
  Let us pray:
    God of light and hope.
    Your strength raised Jesus from the dead,
    so that we could live a life free of sin.
    May you enlighten our innermost vision,
    so that we may celebrate the gifts of the Spirit.
    May our lives always praise you
    as God who lives and reigns forever and ever.

Assembly:
  Amen.

Scripture: John 14:15-17

(Presider invites the assembly to stand and sing an acclamation.)

Presider:
  The Lord be with you.

Assembly:
  And also with you.

Presider:
  A reading from the holy Gospel according to John.

Assembly:
  Glory to you, Lord.

(Presider reads John 7:37-39. After the reading is ended, presider continues:)

Presider:
  The gospel of the Lord.

Assembly:
  Praise to you, Lord Jesus Christ.

(Presider invites the assembly to be seated. The assembly observes a period of silence or hears a short reflection on scripture.)

Psalm 27

(The assembly sings together a setting of Psalm 27.)

(The assembly observes a period of silence.)

Ritual Action

(Begin by playing meditative instrumental music. During the music, light the tapers; you could ask several candidates to come forward, light their tapers and pass the flame to remaining candidates and adults or invite all candidates and adults to come forward to light their tapers from the paschal candle. However this is done, encourage a reverent and solemn atmosphere. When all candles have been lit, sing again the gathering song.)

Presider:
> Gathered here in the light
> and gathered as one community,
> let us renew the promises made at our baptism.

(Lead candidates and adults in the "Renewal of the Baptismal Promises," found in The Sacramentary, *p. 204, New York: Catholic Book Publishing Co., 1985. Or sing together the setting of the baptismal promises "Renewal of Baptismal Promises" by David Haas,* Who Calls You By Name, Volume 1, *Chicago: GIA Publications, 1988, p. 106.)*

Presider:
> Confident that God hears us,
> let us offer the needs of this community:
> For the Church
> as it continues to spread the good news of Christ...

Assembly:
> Let us pray to the Lord.

Presider:
> For all those who lead our governments
> and work for the justice of all people...

Assembly:
> Let us pray to the Lord.

Presider:
For those who are harmed by our insensitivity,
the homeless, the poor and the forgotten...

Assembly:
Let us pray to the Lord.

Presider:
For all who gather here
as we prepare for confirmation...

Assembly:
Let us pray to the Lord.

(At this point, invite candidates and adults to offer spontaneous prayers.)

Presider:
For this parish community
and the needs of those in pain...

Assembly:
Let us pray to the Lord.

Presider:
For the sick
and for those who await death...

Assembly:
Let us pray to the Lord.

Presider:
God of hope and light,
you have bestowed on us in Christ
every spiritual blessing in the heavens.
May we walk as children of light
and bear witness to your truth.
We praise you as the God who lives and reigns for ever and ever.

Assembly:
Amen.

Presider:
The Lord be with you.

Assembly:
And also with you.

Presider:
May almighty God bless us, Father, Son+ and Holy Spirit.

Assembly:
Amen.

Presider:
Let us go forth and walk in the light of Christ.

Assembly:
Thanks be to God.

(Conclude by singing together the gathering song.)

• •

Alternative Closing Prayer
(if not presenting the ritual)

Presider:
God of light and hope,
your strength raised Jesus from the dead,
so that we can live a life free of sin.
May you enlighten our innermost vision,
so that we may celebrate the gifts of the Spirit.
May our lives always praise you
as God who lives and reigns forever and ever.

Assembly:
Amen.

Ritual A: Procession of the Oils
Blessing of Candidates
(if used within the context of a eucharistic assembly)

Presider:
> I invite the candidates for confirmation to come forward.

(After the candidates have come forward, the presider continues:)
> Bow your heads and ask for God's blessing.

(Presider extends hands in blessing over candidates; you may wish to invite others in the assembly to extend their hands as well.)

Presider:
> God of the poor and lowly,
> you sent the Spirit of the Lord
> to announce glad tidings to all.
> Bless these candidates
> as they continue to hear the good news of the Lord.
> Bless these catechists
> as they proclaim the power of Christ Jesus in their lives.
> Bless this assembly
> as we try to live as witnesses of the gospel.
> May our lives be enriched by this journey,
> And may we be blessed, Father, Son and Holy Spirit.

Assembly:
> Amen.

Opening Prayer

(if done at the beginning of the catechetical session)

Presider:
God of the poor and lowly,
you sent the Spirit of the Lord
to announce glad tidings to all.
Be with these candidates
as they continue to hear the good news of the Lord.
Be with these catechists
as they proclaim the power of Christ Jesus in their lives.
May our lives be enriched by this journey,
And may we be blessed, Father, Son and Holy Spirit.

Assembly:
Amen.

• •

Ritual
Materials
Bible
incense
Holy Oils from the ambry (repository) of the church: oil of the sick, oil of the catechumens and holy chrism

Gathering
(Presider invites the assembly to stand and sing one of these gathering songs: "Jesu Tawa Pano/Jesus, We Are Here" by Patrick Matsikenyiri, OCP Publications, "Here I Am, Lord" by Dan Schutte, OCP Publications and New Dawn Music, "God Has Chosen Me" by Bernadette Farrell, OCP Publications, or another song of discipleship or mission.)

Presider:
In the name of the Father, Son and Holy Spirit.

Assembly:
Amen.

Presider:
The Lord be with you.

Assembly:
And also with you.

Presider:
As we come to the close of this session,
we hear the words of God
and acknowledge the Holy Oils of our community.
Let us pray:
God of love and compassion,
you sent the Holy Spirit
to enlighten our minds and our hearts.
May our hearts and minds be open
to the power of your Word.
We praise you
as the God who lives and reigns forever and ever.

Assembly:
Amen.

Scripture: Luke 4:16-22

(Presider invites the assembly to stand and sing an acclamation.)

Presider:
The Lord be with you.

Assembly:
And also with you.

Presider:
A reading from the holy Gospel according to Luke.

Assembly:
Glory to you, Lord.

(Presider reads Luke 4:16-22. After the reading, presider continues:)

Presider:
The gospel of the Lord.

Assembly:
Praise to you, Lord Jesus Christ.

(Presider invites the assembly to be seated. The assembly observes a period of silence or hears a short reflection on scripture.)

Procession of the Holy Oils

Presider:
Each year during Holy Week,
our Bishop blesses oils at the cathedral,
the mother church of the diocese.
Members of our parish received
and brought back these oils
to be used for special rites in our community.

(Soft instrumental music — the song chosen for the gathering — plays underneath as the presider continues:)

Presider:
Oil of the sick:
This oil of the sick
has been blessed by our bishop
for healing the body, mind and soul.
May the sick,
who are anointed with it,
experience the compassion of Christ
and his saving love.*

(Bring forward the vessel of the Oil of the Sick, with incense, as the assembly sings a refrain of the gathering song. Vessel should be enthroned in a prominent place. Music continues as the presider continues:)

Presider:
Oil of catechumens:
This oil of catechumens
has been blessed by our bishop
for the anointing of those
preparing for baptism.
Through this anointing
they are strengthened by Christ
to resist evil in all its forms,
as they prepare for the saving waters of baptism.*

(Bring forward the vessel of the Oil of the Catechumens, with incense, as the assembly sings a refrain of the gathering song. Vessel should be enthroned in a prominent place. Music continues as the presider says:)

Presider:
Holy Chrism:
This holy chrism,
a mixture of olive oil and perfume,
has been consecrated by our bishop
and the priests of our diocese.
It will be used
to anoint infants after baptism
those who are to be confirmed,
bishops and priests at their ordination,
and altars and churches at the time of their dedication.*

(Bring forward the vessel of Holy Chrism, with incense, as the assembly sings a refrain of one of the gathering song. Vessel should be enthroned in a prominent place. Music concludes and presider and assembly are seated. Assembly observes an extended period of silence.)

Presider:
Let us stand
and pray in the words Christ has given us:
Our Father...
For the kingdom, the power and the glory are yours,
now and forever.

Assembly:
  Amen.

Presider:
  The Lord be with you.

Assembly:
  And also with you.

Presider:
  May God bless all of us,
  Father, Son+ and Holy Spirit.

Assembly:
  Amen.

Presider:
  Let us go forth
  and bear witness to the word of God.

Assembly:
  Thanks be to God.

*Excerpts from "The Reception of the Holy Oils" from the *Sacramentary Supplement*
Copyright © 1994 United States Catholic Conference. Adapted and used with per-
mission of the copyright owner. All rights reserved.

● ●

Alternative Closing Prayer
(if not presenting the ritual)

Presider:
  God of love and compassion,
  You sent the Holy Spirit
  to enlighten our minds and our hearts.

May our hearts and minds be open
to the power of your Word.
We praise you
as the God who lives and reigns forever and ever.

Assembly:
Amen.

Ritual B: Blessing with Oil
Blessing of Candidates
(if used within the context of a eucharistic assembly)

Presider:
I invite the candidates for confirmation to come forward.

(After the candidates have come forward, the presider continues:)
Bow your heads and ask for God's blessing.

(Presider extends hands in blessing over candidates; you may wish to invite others in the assembly to extend their hands as well.)

Presider:
God of goodness and truth,
you sent the Holy Spirit
to glorify you and to inspire us.
Bless these candidates
as they continue to open themselves
to the gifts of the Holy Spirit.
Bless their catechists
as they speak of the truth
present in their lives.
And bless this community
as we open our hearts and our minds
to reflect your love.
May we be blessed, Father, Son and Holy Spirit.

Assembly:
Amen.

Opening Prayer
(if used at the beginning of the catechetical session)

Presider:
God of goodness and truth,
you sent the Holy Spirit

to glorify you and to inspire us.
Be with these candidates
as they continue to open themselves
to the gifts of the Holy Spirit.
Be with their catechists
as they speak of the truth
present in their lives.
May we be blessed, Father, Son and Holy Spirit.

Assembly:
Amen.

● ●

Ritual

Materials

Bible
pitcher of unblessed olive oil
one or more small bowls

Gathering

(Sing together a song of social concern, for example, "On Holy Ground" by Donna Pena, GIA Publications, or "Hold Us in Your Mercy/Penitential Litany" by Tom Conry, GIA Publications.)

Presider:
In the name of the Father, Son and Holy Spirit.

Assembly:
Amen.

Presider:
The Lord by with you.

Assembly:
   And also with you.

Presider:
   As we end this session
   we are called to be Christ,
   present with one another.

Penitential Rite

Presider:
   Lord Jesus,
   your love calls us out of darkness.
   Lord, have mercy.

Assembly:
   Lord, have mercy.

Presider:
   Christ Jesus,
   your words are hope for the lowly.
   Christ, have mercy.

Assembly:
   Christ, have mercy.

Presider:
   Lord Jesus,
   your Spirit lifts us from moments of despair.
   Lord, have mercy.

Assembly:
   Lord, have mercy.

Presider:
   May almighty God
   have mercy on us,
   forgive us our sins
   and bring us to everlasting life.

Assembly:
  Amen.

Presider:
  Let us pray:
  God of all hope,
  you sent us your Son
  to show us the ways of peace.
  May we open our hearts
  to all in need,
  And may we always embody
  the healing Spirit of Christ.
  We ask this through Christ our Lord.

Assembly:
  Amen.

Scripture: John 16:5-7, 12-13

(Presider invites the assembly to stand and sing an acclamation.)

Presider:
  The Lord be with you.

Assembly:
  And also with you.

Presider:
  A reading from the holy Gospel according to John.

Assembly:
  Glory to you, Lord.

(Presider reads John 16:5-7, 12-13. After the reading, presider continues:)

Presider:
  The gospel of the Lord.

Assembly:
  Praise to you, Lord Jesus Christ.

(Presider invites the assembly to be seated. The assembly observes a period of silence or hears a short reflection on scripture.)

Ritual Action

(Presider lifts pitcher of oil.)

Presider:
    Blessed are you,
    God of all greatness.
    You have given us oil
    as a sign of healing and strength.
    May this oil remind us
    of our call to heal and forgive one another.

(Presider pours oil into bowl or bowls; offer several stations if you have a large number of candidates and adults. Presider explains:)

    I now invite you to come forward in pairs.
    The first partner in each pair extends hands, palms up.
    Second partner dips fingers into the oil
    and touches fingers to first partner's palms.
    Second partner says,
    "N., may God bless you and always be with you."
    Second partner then lays hands
    on top of first partner's hands, palm down.
    Second partner prays in silence.

(Presider and a catechist may wish to model this for the assembly. When partners have finished, they switch roles and repeat. Throughout the ritual, play music softly, perhaps an instrumental version of the gathering song.)

Presider:
    Let us stand
    and pray in the words Christ has given us:

Assembly:
    Our Father...
    For the kingdom and the power and the glory are yours,
    now and forever.
    Amen.

Presider:
  The Lord be with you.

Assembly:
  And also with you.

Presider:
  May God bless all of us, Father, Son+ and Holy Spirit.

Assembly:
  Amen.

Presider:
  Let us go forth to serve Christ and one another.

Assembly:
  Thanks be to God.

• •

Alternative Closing Prayer
(if not presenting the ritual)

Presider:
  God of all hope,
  you sent us your Son
  to show us the ways of peace.
  May we open our hearts
  to all in need,
  And may we always embody
  the healing Spirit of Christ.
  We ask this through Christ our Lord.

Assembly:
  Amen.

Rituals for Unit

4

Ritual A: Penitential Rite and Sign of Peace
Blessing of Candidates
(if used within the context of a eucharistic assembly)

Presider:
I invite the candidates for confirmation to come forward.

(After the candidates have come forward, the presider continues:)

Bow your heads and ask for God's blessing.

(Presider extends hands in blessing over candidates; you may wish to invite others in the assembly to extend their hands as well.)

Presider:
Exalted and holy God,
you raised Jesus
so that we may know your power over death.
Bless these candidates
as they search for peace in their lives.
Bless their catechists
as they share from their experiences.
Bless this community
as we join in prayer
for those on their journey toward confirmation.
May we all be blessed, Father, Son and Holy Spirit.

Assembly:
Amen.

Opening of Session

(if used at the beginning of the catechetical session)

Presider:
Exalted and holy God,
you raised Jesus
so that we may know your power over death.
Be with these candidates
as they search for peace in their lives.
Be with their catechists
as they share from their experiences.
We ask this through Christ our Lord.

Assembly:
Amen.

• •

Ritual

Note: It would be appropriate at this time to have the candidates attend a parish reconciliation service instead of participating in this prayer service. If candidates have not received the sacrament of reconciliation, they should still participate in the parish celebration of the sacrament.

Materials

Bible

Gathering

(As the assembly gathers, sing together "Prayer for Peace" by David Haas, GIA Publications, or "Litany of the Spirit" by Paul Inwood, OCP Publications.)

Presider:
In the name of the Father, Son and Holy Spirit.

Assembly:
Amen.

Presider:
The Lord be with you.

Assembly:
And also with you.

Penitential Rite

Presider:
As we come to the close of this session,
let us call to mind our need
to be at peace with God and one another.
Lord Jesus,
you bring peace
to those who are unsettled.
Lord, have mercy.

Assembly:
Lord, have mercy.

Presider:
Christ Jesus,
you bring hope
to families lost in despair.
Christ, have mercy.

Assembly:
Christ, have mercy.

Presider:
Lord Jesus,
you call for a peace
in a world often shrouded in violence.
Lord, have mercy.

Assembly:
Lord, have mercy.

Presider:
  May almighty God
  have mercy on us,
  forgive us our sins
  and bring us to everlasting life.

Assembly:
  Amen.

Prayer
Presider:
  Let us pray:
  God of healing and peace,
  the fire of your Spirit
  warms the hearts of those who are cold.
  May we be open to your Word
  and may we live our lives in peace.
  We ask this through Christ our Lord.

Assembly:
  Amen.

Presider:
  Let us be seated for the Word of God.

Scripture: Acts 2:1-6, 14, 22-23, 32-33
*(Presider reads Acts 2:1-6, 14, 22-23, 32-33. After the reading, there may
be silence or a short reflection on scripture.)*

Concluding Rite
Presider:
  Let us now stand
  and join in the words that Christ himself has given us:

Assembly:
  Our Father...
  For the kingdom, the power and the glory are yours,
  now and forever.
  Amen.

Presider:
Lord Jesus Christ,
You said to your apostles:
I leave you peace, my peace I give you.
Look not on our sins, but on the faith of your Church,
and grant us the peace and unity of your kingdom,
where you live for ever and ever.

Assembly:
Amen.

Presider:
The peace of the Lord be with you always.

Assembly:
And also with you.

Presider:
Let us offer each other the sign of peace.*

(The assembly exchanges the sign of peace.)

Presider:
The Lord be with you

Assembly:
And also with you

Presider:
May almighty God bless us.
Our celebration has ended.
Let us go forth in peace
to love and serve our God and one another.

Assembly:
Thanks be to God.

(Conclude by singing again the gathering song.)

*"Sign of Peace," *The Sacramentary.* (New York: Catholic Book Publishing Company, 1985), 562.

Alternative Closing Prayer

(if not presenting the ritual)

Presider:
   God of healing and peace,
   The fire of your Spirit
   warms the hearts of those who are cold.
   May we be open to your Word
   and may we live our lives in peace.
   We ask this through Christ our Lord.

Assembly:
   Amen.

Presider:
   Let us offer each other a sign of peace.

(The assembly exchanges the sign of peace.)

Ritual B: Sprinkling Ritual and Sign of the Cross

Blessing of Candidates

(if done within the context of eucharistic assembly)

Presider:
I invite the candidates for confirmation to come forward.

(After the candidates have come forward, the presider continues:)

Bow your heads and ask for God's blessing.

(Presider extends hands in blessing over candidates; you may wish to invite others in the assembly to extend their hands as well.)

Presider:
God of all that is living,
your son came forth from the waters
to serve the world.
Bless these candidates
as they journey toward the sacrament of confirmation.
Bless their catechists
as they share their stories of faith.
May we hold these members of our assembly
in our prayers.
May their journey inspire us
to remember our call to ongoing conversion.
May we blessed, Father, Son and Holy Spirit.

Assembly:
Amen.

Opening of Session

(if used at the beginning of the catechetical session)

Presider:
God of all that is living,
your son came forth from the waters

to serve the world.
Be with these candidates
as they journey toward the sacrament of confirmation.
Be with their catechists
as they share their stories of faith.
May our journey inspire us
to remember our call to ongoing conversion.
May we be blessed, Father, Son and Holy Spirit.

Assembly:
  Amen.

• •

Ritual
Materials
Bible
candle
matches
asperges branch (wrap dried flowers with floral wire and tape)
large bowl of water
optional: several smaller bowls of water

Note: Arrange the materials on a square table in the center or front
of the assembly. Place the presider's chair to one side of the table.

Gathering
*(As the assembly gathers, stand and sing "Send Us Your Spirit" by David
Haas, GIA Publications, or "Send Out Your Spirit" by Tim Schoenbachler,
OCP Publications.)*

Presider:
  In the name of the Father, Son and Holy Spirit.

Assembly:
  Amen.

Presider:
The peace of Christ be with you.

Assembly:
And also with you.

Presider:
As we come to the end of this session,
let us remember our baptism.

(Presider moves hand through water as following is said:)

Good and gracious God,
tese waters remind us
of the waters that held your son.
From these waters
new life has sprung forth.
We praise you and bless you.

(The assembly sings an acclamation, perhaps a simple alleluia or the refrain of the gathering song.)

Presider:
Your Son, Christ Jesus,
called people to quench their thirst
at the waters.
We have come as a thirsty people
wanting the waters of eternal life.
We praise you and bless you.

(The assembly sings an acclamation, perhaps a simple alleluia or the refrain of the gathering song.)

Presider:
The Holy Spirit
has moved through the waters
giving energy to all life.
We come confident
of the Spirit's power.
We praise you and bless you.

(The assembly sings an acclamation, perhaps a simple alleluia or the refrain of the gathering song.)

Presider:
   May we now be renewed
   in the waters of new life.

(Presider invites the assembly to rise and come forward. Presider uses the asperges branch to sprinkle candidates and adults, who are encouraged to make the sign of the cross as they are sprinkled. For larger assemblies, use several bowls and invite catechists or other adults to sprinkle those in the assembly. During the sprinkling, sing a common refrain familiar to the assembly, perhaps the "Gloria" sung in your parish.)

Presider:
   Let us pray:
   God among us,
   your son was washed
   in the river Jordan.
   May we too be washed anew
   as we make our final preparations for confirmation.
   May we praise you
   as God who lives and reigns
   forever and ever.

Assembly:
   Amen.

Presider:
   Let us be seated for the reading of the scripture.

Scripture: Joel 2:23–3:1-2a

(Presider reads Joel 2:23–3:1-2a. After the reading, there may be silence or a short reflection on scripture.)

Ritual Action

(Play soft music — perhaps an instrumental version of the gathering song. Invite the assembly to stand; all members of the assembly will need room to move about freely. Presider and catechist go to each candidate, signing them in the name of the Father, Son and Holy Spirit. Each parent may also bless

his or her own son or daughter. Likewise, each sponsor may wish to bless his or her own candidate. When all candidates have been signed and blessed, continue:)

Presider:
Let us pray in the words Christ has given us:

Assembly:
Our Father…
For the kingdom, the power and the glory are yours,
now and forever.
Amen.

Presider:
The Lord be with you.

Assembly:
And also with you.

Presider:
May God bless all of us, Father, Son+ and Holy Spirit.

Assembly:
Amen.

Presider:
Let us go forth
renewed in the waters of baptism.

Assembly:
Thanks be to God.

(Conclude by singing the gathering song.)

• •

Alternative Closing Prayer

(if not presenting the ritual)

Presider:
God among us,
your son was washed
in the river Jordan.
May we too be washed anew
as we make our final preparations for confirmation.
May we praise you
as God who lives and reigns
forever and ever.

Assembly:
Amen.

Preparing for the Rite: An Overview
Purpose of this Overview

This overview—written for liturgy committees, catechetical groups, parish staffs—offers a walk-through of the rite of confirmation for sponsors and parents. We recommend that the rehearsal for the sacrament take place *without* the candidates, allowing them to come to the sacrament with an enhanced sense of awe and wonder. Candidates have already experienced the ritual actions and lectionary readings of the rite in the catechetical gatherings. These elements appropriately come together for the first time during the celebration.

Directly prior to the sacrament, spend time with candidates going over the acclamations and actions of the eucharistic liturgy. (Hopefully, candidates have been attending liturgy on a regular basis and are already familiar with the acclamations and actions.) A simple review also offers an opportunity to answer questions candidates may have about the primary expression of our faith—the celebration of the eucharistic meal.

Important note: Check with your own diocese on directives for the celebration of the sacrament. Each diocese has its own expectations and guidelines—please follow these! To obtain these guidelines, contact your ordinary's office or the diocesan office of worship. It is also helpful if those working on the liturgy are familiar with the Church's liturgical documents, especially:

- *Constitution on the Sacred Liturgy*
- *General Instruction of the Roman Missal*
- *Ceremonial of Bishops*
- *Music in Catholic Worship*
- *Liturgical Music Today*

These documents offer specific paragraphs on confirmation and principles of good liturgy. These can be obtained from United States Catholic Conference of Bishops (USCC), 3211 Fourth St., N.E., Washington, D.C. 20017-1194, 1-202-541-3000, or in a handy, one-volume book, *The Liturgy Documents: A Parish Resource* (Third Edition) published by Liturgy Training Publications, 1800 N. Hermitage Ave., Chicago, Illinois, 60622-1101, 1-800-933-1800.

The following are pastoral *suggestions* for celebrating the rites, *not* rules. We offer them as starting points for a discussion of the rite; adapt, as necessary, for specific situation.

Preparation of the Candidates

To what extent should candidates be involved in preparing the sacrament? While we understand that having candidates help prepare the liturgy increases their "ownership," we question their ability to uphold the documents of the Church. Instead, we suggest spending time with them in the week prior to the rite talking about their journey toward the sacrament. Discuss the following questions; then, as you prepare the liturgy, draw from the lived experience of the candidates as reflected in their answers.

Questions for Candidates:
- What images stand out for you in your preparation for confirmation?
- What scripture(s) most resonate with your preparation?
- What words stand out for you in your preparation?
- How would you picture your celebration of the sacrament?
- Who do you feel needs to be present at the celebration?

When asking these questions, please stress that there are no right or wrong answers. You might simply explain that you are "doing some research." If necessary, review each of the sessions and briefly summarize and reflect on the various scriptures and activities.

Preparing for the Rite

The rite of confirmation is, above all else, a celebration of the *community*; let it look and feel like a typical parish liturgy. So often we make this celebration "different" from our usual celebration. Keep in mind, as you read the ideas in this section, that you are urged to incorporate them in the light of how you *already* celebrate liturgy in the community. These ideas might be the impetus for changes within your regular celebration.

Who Should Be Present?

Ideally, members of the worshiping community should be present, since the rite will take place at a regularly scheduled liturgy. If the rite does *not* take place at a regular liturgy, then be sure to extend an invitation to the entire parish. Often, this celebration draws a large number of guests; how welcoming of the parish to provide hospitality by having a large number of parishioners present as well!

Environment

This is a day of celebration. If celebrating outside of the lenten season, create a festive space. Think beyond flowers (which are wonderful!):

- Process in with festive banners of brightly colored fabric; plain banners—without fabric words or symbols—are very effective.
- Hang colorful mobiles, some at the front of the church, some over the assembly.
- Use candles of different sizes and shapes, some stationary and others carried in procession during the gathering song.

Music

Again, remember that this is a *parish* celebration: What music does the assembly know? This may not be the best time to introduce new music, unless it is "instant" music—music that a cantor can sing and to which the assembly can easily respond. Nor is this the time for a choir "performance," one step removed form the assembly. If used, the choir should enhance the assembly's singing.

Keep in mind, too, that many visitors will attend. We therefore recommend selecting songs and hymns that known to a wider cross-section of people. A nice song may be lost if it's unknown.

Review of the Rite

Suggestions for the celebration of confirmation are found in *The Sacramentary*, pages 834-837 (New York: Catholic Book Publishing Co., 1985). Please note the following guideline on page 834:

One of the following Masses is celebrated when confirmation is given within Mass or immediately before or after it, except on Sundays of Advent, Lent, and Easter, solemnities, Ash Wednesday, and the weekdays of Holy Week. Red or white vestments are worn.

Please adhere to this statement. Note that Sunday celebration of the sacrament calls us to attend to how the parish celebrates that Sunday liturgy. Ask yourself:

- Could this be the only celebration of the eucharist our parish has this day?

Gathering Rites

Use instruments and procession to enhance the gathering song or hymn. Consider moving throughout the entire space, not just down one aisle; imagine the inspiration as banners, flowers and candles as they flow from and around all directions.

Candidates do not need to process into the space; they are already part of the assembly and should be seated with them. You might invite selected candidates to carry the banners, flowers and candles. Check local directives if a deacon participates. The use of incense in the entrance procession adds dignity.

Introductory Rites

These are from the mass of the day. If a local ordinary presides, the pastor or confirmation coordinator may want to formally welcome the ordinary to the assembly. Outside of the Easter season, a sprinkling rite would be appropriate.

Opening Prayer

There are four options for opening prayer given in *The Sacramentary* (New York: Catholic Book Publishing Co., 1985). We like the opening prayer in option B (p. 836), which is simple, yet calls us to walk and grow in faith.

Readings

See lectionary options 763-767 (*Lectionary for Mass*, New York: Catholic Book Publishing Co., 1974, pp. 915-925). These readings were covered within the catechetical sessions. Which did you find most appropriate for your specific group of candidates? During Advent, Lent and Easter, solemnities, Ash Wednesday and the weekdays of Holy Week, use the readings of the day.

Homily

Paragraph 21 of the "Rite of Confirmation" (*The Rites of the Catholic Church, Volume One.* Collegeville, Minn., 1990, pp. 469-515) describes the presentation of candidates prior to the homily. If the number of candidates is not too great, consider naming each candidate individually; this can be done by the "pastor, or another priest, deacon, or catechist." The presiding bishop gives the homily.

Renewal of Baptismal Promises
Paragraph 23 of the "Rite of Confirmation" provides the formula for asking the candidates to renew their baptismal promises. Sing the response if this is a practice in your community.

The Laying on of Hands
During the laying on of hands (paras. 24-25, "Rite of Confirmation"), we find it meaningful for the candidates to kneel and the assembly to stand. The bishop and concelebrating priests first pray a prayer. A moment of silence follows the prayer. "The bishop and the priests who will minister the sacrament with him lay hands upon all the candidates (by extending their hands over them)" (para. 25, "Rite of Confirmation").

The Anointing with Chrism
For the anointing with the chrism (paras. 26-29, "Rite of Confirmation"), the candidates and sponsors come forward to the bishop. Each sponsor leads his or her candidate. If an introduction has not taken place this would be an appropriate time for the sponsor to introduce candidates to the bishop. The sponsor lays his or her right hand on the shoulder of the candidate. Candidates should know in advance this exchange:
- Bishop: "N., be sealed with the Gift of the Holy Spirit."
- Candidate: "*Amen.*"
- Bishop: "Peace be with you."
- Candidate: "And also with you."

If this invitation has been a frequent part of the preparation rituals, you will probably not need to rehearse it with candidates.

During this time, play music if this is your custom. Background music could be performed by woodwind and keyboard, with perhaps a soft mantra done by the choir. This allows the assembly to take part, yet still attend to the rite.

General Intercession

There is no profession of faith. Prayers of the faithful (para. 30, "Rite of Confirmation") need to be written to honor the context of the community praying. Remember the order:

- the Church
- world leaders
- those oppressed
- local needs
- the sick
- the dying

Please avoid making the intercessions into mini-homilies; keep them brief and to the point.

Preparation of Gifts

It would be appropriate to take up a collection; if not for the parish, perhaps for a local need that the candidates are aware of.

The setting of the table is a lovely gesture here. Perhaps candidates or members of the parish can take part in this. The gifts that are brought forward are only the bread and wine to be used at this eucharist, and the collection for the needy. No other things need to be placed on the altar. The procession could be led with candles and incense, if customary.

Follow the Order of the Mass as prescribed by the rubrics of *The Sacramentary*, pages 834-837 (New York: Catholic Book Publishing Co., 1985). Again, the liturgy should reflect the local assembly in the use of acclamations. Great care should be given to the communion rite. This is not an afterthought to the anointing with chrism. Do not rush; create an atmosphere of great reverence. Appropriate music would include songs that are either mantra in style or that have easy refrains; let the assembly come forward singing without the use of books or worship aids.

After communion, observe a period of silence. Avoid intruding with a spoken or a sung reflection. Much has happened; allow the assembly to sit silently, reflecting in the presence of God.

The bishop offers a solemn blessing or prayer over the people (para. 33, "Rite of Confirmation"). See the directives for your specific situation.

The concluding music does not have to be a congregational hymn, although one would truly be a fitting conclusion to this liturgy. A song with a simple refrain or repetition could be used. Think in terms of procession. Consider having the entire assembly process to another space for a reception. Use candles and banners in the reception area.

Overall, think of this celebration as a community welcoming the candidates into a deeper part of their faith. Let the liturgy embody this.

PART TWO: Retreats for Confirmation

Introduction to the Retreats

For centuries, people preparing for significant religious events have taken time out of their ordinary lives to "retreat." Scripture tells us that Jesus often went away by himself to pray. Getting away from daily distractions and pressures allows us to focus, listen, pray and grow, both as individuals and as a community of believers.

In addition to weekly faith formation experiences, retreats can provide candidates with additional opportunities for community building and reflection. When a group of candidates gathers for a confirmation retreat, they gather as a community of baptized believers seeking to recognize the living presence of God in their midst. For some young people, retreats affirm what they already experience in their parish communities. For others, retreats serve as significant experiences of what it means to be part of a spiritual community of faith. For all who gather, a well-planned retreat can provide three things:

- an opportunity to get to know other members of the community
- a deepening of a candidate's understanding of his or her own gift-edness
- an opportunity to deepen one's relationship with God

What follows in this section are two confirmation retreat models, tailored to meet the spiritual and developmental needs of various age groups. For each retreat, a "Schedule Overview" is followed by detailed "Activity Descriptions" for suggested activities. The "Activity Descriptions" include two sections:

- Prepare the Activity (including which materials to gather)
- Lead the Activity

These descriptions provide retreat planners and facilitators with the necessary information needed to effectively lead the retreat.

Gifts of the Spirit (pp. 71-80) is a one-day model designed to be used early in the process. **Gifts of the Spirit** invites participants to focus on two questions:

- Who am I?
- How do I see the Spirit expressed in myself and in the community around me?

You will find two versions of the **Gifts of the Spirit** retreat, one for younger candidates (roughly ages 7-12), and one for older candidates (roughly ages 13-17). Choose the version most appropriate for your group.

Both versions of the retreat incorporate community-building, creative expression, panel and small-group discussions and personal reflection time. While designed to be offered for a group of candidates, the retreats could be adapted for us with candidates and their parents or sponsors with some modifications.

Create in Me is a more in-depth retreat, which works effectively once candidates know one another. It is designed to be used in the middle of the confirmation process or toward the end as a final time of reflection before the sacrament. There are three versions of the **Create in Me** retreat (pp. 81-109):

- a day-long retreat for younger candidates (pp. 81-86)
- an overnight retreat for junior-high candidates (pp. 87-109)
- an overnight retreat for high-school candidates (pp. 87-109)

Central to the theme of **Create in Me** is the exploration of how individuals have been created in the image and likeness of God. The activities include mask-making, guided imagery, ritual, reflection on "rites of passage," community-building, small-group discussions and panel discussions.

To effectively use the retreats in this book, *plan thoroughly, employ competent leaders and allow the Spirit to work.* We offer the following hints as you begin your preparation:

Select a Site and Date

Select a few dates that do not conflict with parish, school or community calendars. Begin contacting retreat facilities nine months to a year in advance of your desired retreat date. When choosing a facility, keep in mind the size of your group, the cost per person, small and large group meeting room spaces, prayer space, food service/cooking facilities, sleeping accommodations, recreation options, and the distance of the facility from your parish. Once you have selected a date and a site, make this information available to candidates and their parents as early as possible to avoid conflicts later.

Form the Team

The retreats in this book are designed for *team* facilitation. Team leaders can include both youth and adults who are willing to assist the retreat coordinator in planning and implementing the retreat. When selecting leaders, develop a balanced team with a variety of personalities and talents. From the outset, clarify, in writing, your expectations of each team member.

Train the Team

How do you develop competent and confident team members? You train them. Training takes place in a series of meetings prior to the retreat, focusing on the following:
- team building
- small and large group facilitation
- prayer leadership
- adolescent faith development
- storytelling
- specific activity leadership

If your diocese has a child abuse policy, provide this important information and training for your leaders.

Gather Supplies

Begin gathering supplies several weeks before the retreat. Leaving this task to the last minute almost always causes frustration and guarantees that you will forget something. Use the Materials Needed sections of the Activity Descriptions when developing a supply list.

Be Creative

Do not be afraid to bring your own creativity and the talents of your team to the retreats in this book. While the activities are effective if led as written, variations can emerge which might better meet the needs of your particular candidates.

Evaluate

Establish a date when you will regather the team after the retreat to reflect on the experience. This evaluation allows you to assess what went well and what you want to change for future retreats.

Trust the Spirit

Once the planning and preparations for the retreat are complete, the coordinator and retreat team must allow the Spirit to work in and among those gathered. Be open to surprises! Things rarely go exactly as planned, but that does not mean you were ineffective.

While the retreat coordinator and team members are in a "servant leadership" role, allow time for their personal prayer and reflection during the retreat.

The gifts *(charisms)* of the Spirit are visible in each member of the community of faith. Each individual is made in the image and likeness of God. May your experience of planning and leading a retreat for your confirmation candidates affirm your own giftedness and deepen your faith in your Creator.

Gifts of the Spirit

One-Day Retreat for Younger Candidates (roughly ages 7-12)

8:00 am	Team Arrives for Set-Up and Team Meeting
9:00 am	Candidates Arrive: Distribute Name Tags
9:10 am	Welcome: Team Introductions, Rules, Overview of the Day
9:25 am	Community-Building Session (p. 72)
10:00 am	Witness Talk: "Personal Gifts" (p. 73)
10:10 am	Small Group: "Who Am I?" (p. 74)
11:00 am	Snack Break; Brief Team Check-In
11:10 am	Regather Group
11:15 am	Panel or Fish-Bowl Discussion: Gifts of the Spirit (p. 76)
12:00 pm	Lunch
12:30 pm	Small Group: "Expressions of the Spirit" (p. 77)
1:25 pm	Regather in Large Group
1:30 pm	Prayer Service (p. 78)
2:00 pm	Retreat Ends

One-Day Retreat for Older Candidates (roughly ages 13-17)

8:00 am	Team Arrives for Set-Up and Team Meeting
9:00 am	Candidates Arrive: Distribute Name Tags
9:10 am	Welcome: Team Introductions, Rules, Overview of the Day
9:25 am	Community-Building Session (p. 72)
10:00 am	Witness Talk: "Personal Gifts" (p. 73)
10:10 am	Small Group: "I Am..." (p. 75)
10:25 am	Small-Group Sharing
11:00 am	Snack Break; Brief Team Check-In
11:15 am	Panel or Fish-Bowl Discussion: Gifts of the Spirit (p. 76)

12:00 pm	Lunch
12:30 pm	Small Group: "Expressions of the Spirit" (p. 77)
1:15 pm	Prayer Service (p. 78)
2:00 pm	Retreat Ends

Retreat Activities

Community-Building Session *(for both Younger and Older Candidates)*

A well-planned community-building session helps participants feel comfortable with other retreatants as well as the retreat team. It also helps the team gain an overall sense of the group. If necessary, the team members can meet briefly after this session to make adjustments to the schedule based on their observations.

To **prepare the session:**
Choose your activities from a community-building resource; see the bibliography at the end of this book (p. 110).

When choosing activities for the community-building session, take into account:

- *Size and nature of the group:* How large is the group? How long have group members known one another? Have any new members been added to the group? How much community-building has been done prior to the retreat? Are there any external circumstances which could effect the group's interaction (e.g., exam week, recent death of a classmate, mandatory nature of a retreat, prom time)? How will you handle persons with physical limitations who might be unable to participate in some of the activities? Is there an even or odd number of participants? (Note: If pairs are necessary, have a team member step in or out to even things up.) Most community building, icebreaker or crowdbreaker books will indicate the appropriate number of participants for each activity.
- *Size and nature of the space:* Will the room you have selected accommodate the kinds of activities you have planned? How does the room need to be arranged prior to the group's arrival? Who is responsible for room set-up? If the room is large, is a sound system available so that the leaders can be heard? Is the room carpeted? Where are the heating and air-conditioning controls? Which team member will be responsible for monitoring room temperature as the session progresses?

- *The overall retreat plan:* What are your goals for this session? Have you included a mixture of activities (e.g., large and small group, verbal and non-verbal)? Are any of the activities competitive (something to avoid if one of your goals is to build community in the large group)? How well does the session flow? Does it move from a minimal "threat level" to a deeper level of interaction? Have you selected competent team members to lead the session? Have team members had an opportunity to practice leading the activities prior to the retreat?
- *The community-building activity itself:* Clear and simple directions given by leaders are crucial to the success of this session. It is important that leaders are confident and prepared. Participants sense when a leader feels insecure and tentative, and respond accordingly. Watch the group and the clock throughout the session; make adjustments as necessary.
- *Processing after the activity:* After the last activity of the community building session, take a few minutes to "process" the experience with the group before continuing with the retreat. A few questions the leader might ask include:
  — Which activity was the most fun?
  — Which was the easiest? most difficult?
  — Did you gain any new insights about yourself? about the group?
  — Why do we start a retreat with a session like this?
  — How can we, as a community, carry what we have learned into the rest of the retreat?

Witness Talk: Personal Gifts *(for both Younger and Older Candidates)*

To **prepare the talk:**

Decide which member of the retreat team will deliver the talk. In the "Witness Talk," the speaker introduces the retreat theme of "personal giftedness and uniqueness." For the talk, the speaker:
- names some of his or her own "gifts of the Spirit"
- describes how he or she uses these gifts to help others
- cites several brief stories which exemplify the use of his or her gifts

It is important with this age group to distinguish between "naming and claiming gifts" and "bragging." For further help in preparing this talk, see the *Confirmation: Anointed and Sealed with the Spirit Leader's Guide*, pages 39-41.

"Who Am I?" *(for Younger Candidates only)*

To **prepare the activity**:

Gather materials:
- 8½" x 11" blank, white paper
- magazines and newspapers (Collect a variety of magazines with pictures with which candidates could identify, for example, "Sports Illustrated," "People" and "Seventeen.")
- newspapers
- glue
- scissors
- markers

To **lead the activity**:

Divide participants into small groups. Small-group leaders then lead a brief discussion on the "Witness Talk" just given:
- How can we relate to what *(Name)* was saying about gifts *(charisms)* of the Spirit?
- How and where do we see the Spirit working in the world?
- In what ways do we see the Spirit working in the members of our families? in our friends?
- Name an example of the Spirit's presence in you.

After the discussion, offer these directions:
- Search through magazines and newspapers to find symbols of the Spirit's presence in your life.
- Find as many images as possible, then create a collage of the images on paper.
- Think about all aspects of your life as you seek to identify the presence of the Spirit within you.
- You'll be sharing your collages with the other members of your small group.

Allow time for candidates to finish their collages and share them in their groups.

"I Am..." *(for Older Candidates only)*

To **prepare the activity:**
Gather materials:
- paper
- felt-tip markers or pencils

To **lead the activity:**
Divide participants into small groups. Distribute paper and markers or pencils.

Ask each candidate to write his or her name on one side of a piece of paper, then, on the other side of the paper, to write the words "I Am..." in large letters.

Share with candidates some of the "I am" statements from the Gospel of John that describe Jesus, for example:
- I am the bread of life.
- I am the good shepherd.
- I am the light of the world.
- I am the way, the truth and the life.

Explain that other people get to know us—and we can get to know ourselves better—by simply finishing our own "I am..." statements. Give candidates five to seven minutes to brainstorm as many personal completions to the "I am..." statement as they can. Encourage them to fill the paper with words describing who they are, for example:
- I am...a sister (brother).
- I am...an aunt (uncle).
- I am...an only child.
- I am...a soccer player.
- I am...afraid.
- I am...a lot of fun.
- I am...an artist.

After five to seven minutes, invite group members to read their statements to the other members of their small groups.

When all have had an opportunity to share, invite them to look back at their paper and to circle:

- the statement that means the most to them
- the statement that means the least to them
- the statement they find most surprising

If time permits, invite them also to share these reflections with their small groups.

Panel or Fish-Bowl Discussion: "What Is Confirmation?" *(for both Younger and Older Candidates)*

To **prepare the discussion:**

First, decide whether to conduct a panel discussion or a fish-bowl discussion:

- In a panel discussion, the facilitator and panel members sit in front of the group. Panel members remain the same throughout the discussion.
- In a fish-bowl discussion, the facilitator and panel members sit in a circle within the circle of the larger group. Throughout the discussion, any group member may "tag" a panel member; the tagged panel member then leaves the discussion circle, and the tagging group member take his or her place in the "fish bowl." The fish-bowl discussion may be particularly appropriate for Older Candidates.

Second, select a facilitator and recruit several volunteers to serve as panel members. Parents, sponsors and team members can all serve in this role, or other confirmed members of the parish. You might also consider including someone close in age to the candidates. Provide panel members with the questions the facilitator will use to start the discussion, for example:

- What do you remember most about your confirmation?
- How did you select your sponsor?
- What was your understanding of the sacrament when you were preparing for confirmation?
- How has your understanding of confirmation changed in the years since your confirmation?

Provide these additional, more challenging questions if leading a retreat *for Older Candidates:*

- When have you experienced the gifts of the Spirit in your life?

- In which scripture stories do you most clearly recognize the presence of the Spirit?
- Name a current social issue involving some type of struggle, for example, racism, sexism, unemployment, homelessness, etc. Where in this struggle do you see the presence of God's Spirit? Which gifts of the Spirit do you think would help this situation?
- If you could ask God to send the Spirit today into one area of your life, what area would that be and why? What gift of the Spirit do you most need and why?

To **lead the discussion:**
Introduce the facilitator and the members of the panel. Conduct the discussion, following these ground rules:
- The questions the facilitator asks are intended to get the discussion rolling. Everyone on the panel does not need to answer all the questions.
- The facilitator will also invite questions from candidates and direct them to members of the panel.
- Remember, this is a panel discussion, not a debate. Panel members have been invited to participate so they can share their experiences and their wisdom.
- If the discussion begins to go off on a tangent, it's the facilitator's job to refocus it.
- *For the fish-bowl discussion:* Give current panel members a chance to express their feelings and ideas before tagging them to switch out of the discussion circle.

Expressions of the Spirit *(for both Younger and Older Candidates)*
To **prepare the activity:**
First, gather materials:
- chalkboard or newsprint
- tape or CD Player
- art supplies: scissors, glue, paints, construction paper, felt markers, magazines and newspapers, etc.
- miscellaneous props: items of clothing, dishes, instruments, books, toys, etc.
- Bibles

Second, based on the number of small groups you anticipate having, determine that many different methods groups can use to express the gifts of the Spirit. For example, if you expect to have six groups, you might use these six methods of expression: skit, TV commercial, billboard, song, poem, newspaper or magazine advertisement. Write each of these methods on a separate slip of paper. Arrange the art supplies and props on a table in the meeting space.

To **lead the activity**:
Introduce the activity by reading aloud 1 Corinthians 12:4-13.

Invite the group to brainstorm the gifts *(charisms)* of the Spirit which are present in the gathered community. List these on chalkboard or newsprint.

Divide participants into smaller groups. Explain that each small group will work together to develop a short presentation for the larger group, a presentation that expresses the activity of the Spirit within the community. Encourage them to be very creative, using each other as resources as well as the art supplies and props provided.

Ask each small group leader to come forward to select one of the slips on which you've written a method of expression. Inform each group that they will have 30-40 minutes to complete their project using their assigned method.

When groups have finished, regather for the closing prayer. The small-group presentations will be offered during the prayer.

Prayer Service *(for both Younger and Older Candidates)*

To **prepare the prayer service**:
Gather materials:
- Bible
- candle
- matches
- small table
- cloth
- "Expressions of the Spirit" props and completed projects

At one end of the room, place the candle, the matches and the Bible (open to 1 Corinthians 12:4-13) on the small table, covered with the cloth.

Select a few songs that the group can sing during the prayer service. The songs should be expressive of God's gift of the Spirit to the community of believers.

To **lead the prayer service**:
(Gather in a semicircle around the candle and Bible. The presider removes the cloth and lights the candle.)

Opening Song(s)

Opening Prayer

> *Presider:*
> Loving God, we come to you at the end of our time of retreat. We stand in gratitude for the abundance of grace which you have showered upon us. Help us to continue to recognize the gift of your Spirit present among us and within us. We pray this prayer in the name of Jesus, our brother.

> *All:*
> Amen.

Scripture: 1 Corinthians 12:4-13

Reflection *(Presider or another team member leads a brief reflection on the scripture passage.)*

"Expressions of the Spirit" Reflection *(Small groups present their "Expressions of the Spirit" projects.)*

Lord's Prayer

Closing Prayer *(for Younger Candidates only)*

> *Presider:*
> Gracious God, we stand in your presence, ready to go out into the world to proclaim the Good News. Send us your Spirit, that we may be strengthened in body, mind and soul to be living witness of your love to all those we meet. We pray this prayer in the name of Jesus, our brother.

All:
Amen.

Closing Prayer *(for Older Candidates only)*

Presider:
We stand here at the close of our day together and take a moment to give thanks to God for the many gifts which have been given us. We also stand as a community in need of God's reassuring presence.

(Presider takes candle from table and explains:)

Presider:
I will pass the candle around the circle. When the candle comes to you, you are invited to say a word of thanks to God for the gifts you have received, or to place before God and this community an area of need or concern. If, when the candle reaches you, you wish to remain silent, I ask that you simply hold the candle for a moment as the community prays for you. I will begin...

(Presider prays, then passes the candle to the person on his or her left. When the candle returns to the presider, he or she prays:)

Presider:
Gracious God, we stand in you presence, ready to go out into the world to proclaim the Good News. Send us your Spirit, that we may be strengthened in body, mind and soul to be living witness of your love to all those we meet. We pray this prayer in the name of Jesus, our brother.

All:
Amen.

Closing Song(s)

Create in Me

One-Day Retreat for Younger Candidates

8:00 am	Team Arrives on Site for Set-Up and Team Meeting
9:00 am	Candidates Arrive: Distribute Name Tags
9:00 am	Welcome: Team Introductions, Rules and Overview of the Day
9:10 am	Community-Building Session (p. 72)
9:30 am	Reading of the Creation Story: Genesis 1:1-31
9:40 am	Small Groups: My Own Story (p. 81)
10:30 am	Break
10:45 am	Large Group: Made in the Image and Likeness: Mask-Making (p. 82)
11:30 am	Lunch
12:00 pm	Recreation Break
12:15 pm	Small Groups: Gifts of the Spirit (p. 83)
1:45 pm	Large Group: Letters to God (p. 84)
1:30 pm	Prayer Service
2:00 pm	Retreat Ends

Retreat Activities

My Own Story

To **prepare the activity:**

Gather materials:

8½" x 11" blank, white paper, 2 per participant

crayons

pencils

stapler or yarn and scissors

For each candidate, fold two sheets of blank paper in half to make an eight-page, 5½" x 8½" booklet; staple the fold or tie together with a piece of yarn.

To **lead the activity:**
Distribute the booklets prepared before the retreat. Divide participants into small groups.

Each small-group leader introduces the activity by briefly reviewing the creation story. Small-group leaders invite their group members to decorate the front covers of their booklet by writing "The Story of *(Name),*" using their own names to complete the title. Group members label the next page of their booklets (the inside of the front cover) *Day One*. They continue labeling the pages *Day Two, Day Three,* etc., until the final page (back cover) is labeled *Day Seven*. Group leaders then explain:

- Go back to the page labeled *Day One* and draw a picture of your family when you were first born.
- On *Day Two* draw a picture of your baptism.
- On *Day Three* draw a picture of your first day of school.
- On *Day Four* draw a picture of your first communion.
- On *Day Five* draw a picture of your family now.
- On *Day Six* draw a picture of yourself doing an activity that you like to do.
- On *Day Seven* draw a picture of what you think God looks like.

Allow ten to fifteen minutes at the end of the activity for small-group members to share their completed booklets with their groups.

Made in The Image And Likeness: Paper Masks

To **prepare the activity:**
Gather materials:
- sturdy paper plates
- paint stirrers or tongue depressors
- heavy tape
- small mirrors
- crayons
- scissors
- colored construction paper
- glue
- miscellaneous art supplies

Using heavy tape, attach a paint stirrer or tongue depressor to the back of each paper plate, creating the foundation of the mask. Prepare one mask for each participant.

To **lead the activity:**
Distribute a mirror and one paper-plate mask to each participant. Invite participants to look around the room and notice the similarities among those present. Point out that while some people might have the same hair color or eye color, no two people are exactly the same.

Now ask participants to look into the mirror and notice their *own* features. Ask:
• What do you see when you look in the mirror?

Invite participants to make masks of their own faces using the provided art supplies. They may look into their mirrors to capture as many features as they can that are unique to their faces. Ask them also to cut small holes for eyes. Team members move through the room to assist and encourage the candidates as they work.

When the masks are completed and the supplies have been cleaned up, invite candidates to form a circle and place their masks in front of their faces. Ask everyone to move slowly around the room, guessing to see who is behind each mask.
At the conclusion of this "parade of masks," discuss:
• What do you think God's mask would look like if God made a mask.

Close the activity by asking participants to place their masks aside for later use.

Gifts of the Spirit
To **prepare the activity:**
Gather materials:
• single hole punch, 1 per small group
• 8" pieces of ribbon or yarn, 7 per participant
• colored construction paper
• pens or pencils, 1 per participant
• masks created earlier in the day

To **lead the activity:**
Return to the small groups. Small-group leader asks participants to name some of the gifts of the Spirit. Discuss examples of how they currently see these gifts in their own lives or in the lives of others.

After several minutes of discussion, leaders distribute pencils, ribbon and construction paper, then invite group members to think of seven areas in their lives in which they would like the help of God's Spirit. In other words, if they could ask God to help them with seven things, what would these be? As they think of these areas, ask them to write each one on a piece of construction paper or to cut out a symbol that represents that need, for example, a cut-out capital A could represent the need for help with grades.

The small-group leader then passes the hole punch around the group and asks each candidate to punch seven holes in their mask and one hole in each of their pieces of construction paper.

Participants then tie one end of each of their pieces of ribbon or yarn through the holes on the mask. They tie the other end of each piece of ribbon or yarn to a separate piece of their construction paper.

If time permits, ask volunteers to name and explain one or two of the symbols, words or phrases that they have now added to their masks.

Letters to God

To **prepare the activity:**
Gather materials
• pens or pencils
• paper

To **lead the activity:**
Regather the large group and give each participant a pen or pencil and a sheet of paper. Explain:

• If you could send a letter to God, what would you write?
• Would you thank God for something? ask God for something? just share with God something that has happened to you?
• Write a letter to God right now. When you've finished, sign your letter.

Give participants time to complete their letters. When they've finished, encourage them to take their letters home and share them with their families.

Gather together in a large circle for the Prayer Service.

Prayer Service

To **prepare the service:**
Gather materials:
- candle
- matches
- masks created earlier in the retreat

Select a song or short refrain about God's love, creation or the Spirit that candidates can sing without using songbooks or songsheets.

To **lead the service:**
(Begin by lighting the candle.)

Presider:
Let us begin in the name of the Father and of the Son and of the Holy Spirit.

All:
Amen.

Presider:
Good and loving God, we come to you at the end of our retreat day. We take this time to thank you for your presence with us today and to bring the needs of our hearts to you. Please send us your Spirit so that we may continue to love you and praise you. We pray this prayer in the name of Jesus, our brother and our friend.

All:
Amen.

Presider:
I would like each of you to look at the mask you made today. In your small groups, you had an opportunity to write some words or cut out some symbols of the areas in which you need God's help. Choose one of those words or symbols to share with the group.

After each person shares their word or symbol, we will respond together, "Lord, send us your Spirit." I will begin; then we will move around the circle starting with the person on my left. Listen carefully so that you can really pray for each other.

Presider:
Let us join our hands and pray together the Lord's Prayer.

Lord's Prayer

Closing Prayer

Presider:
Wonderful God, we have come to the end of our retreat day. Take care of us as we leave here. Protect us and all of those that we love. Send your Spirit to help us take care of ourselves, each other and all of your creation. We ask this in the name of Jesus, our brother and our friend.

All:
Amen.

Closing Song

Create in Me

Overnight Retreat for Junior-High Candidates

Friday

4:30 pm	Team Arrives on Site for Set-Up
6:00 pm	Candidates Arrive: Room Assignments, Name Tags
6:15 pm	Welcome, Team Introductions, Rules and Brief Overview of Retreat
6:30 pm	Community-Building Session (p. 72)
7:30 pm	Small Groups: Who We Are (p. 89)
7:45 pm	Small Groups: Hopes and Expectations (p. 89)
8:00 pm	Large Group: Small-Group Reports (p. 90)
8:15 pm	Break
8:30 pm	Small Groups: "I Am..." (p. 91)
9:00 pm	Large Group: Made in the Image and Likeness—Masks (p. 93)
10:30 pm	Break
11:00 pm	Night Prayer: Guided Imagery (p. 97)
11:15 pm	Bedtime
11:30 pm	Lights Out

Saturday

8:30 am	Wake Up
9:00 am	Breakfast
9:30 am	More Community Building (p. 72)
9:45 am	Morning Prayer (p. 101)
10:00 am	Journaling: The Story of Creation / The Story of the Candidate (p. 92)
11:00 am	Break
11:15 am	Journal Reflection and Mask-Decorating (p. 103)
12:30 pm	Lunch
1:00 pm	Free Time
1:30 pm	Panel or Fish-Bowl Discussion of Confirmation (p. 76)
2:15 pm	Small Groups: Grace—The Gift of the Spirit (p. 105)
3:00 pm	Break: Pack Personal Belongings
3:20 pm	Prayer Service (p. 106)
4:00 pm	Retreat Ends

Overnight Retreat for High-School Candidates

Friday Evening

4:30 pm	Team Arrives on Site for Set-Up and Team Meeting
6:00 pm	Candidates Arrive: Room Assignments, Name Tags
6:15 pm	Welcome, Team Introductions, Rules and Brief Overview of Retreat
6:30 pm	Community-Building Session (p. 72)
7:30 pm	Small Groups: Who We Are (p. 89)
7:45 pm	Small Groups: Hopes and Expectations (p. 89)
8:00 pm	Large Group: Small-Group Reports (p. 90)
8:15 pm	Journaling: The Story of Creation/The Story of the Candidate (p. 92)
9:00 pm	Break
9:15 pm	Large Group: Made in the Image and Likeness—Masks (p. 93)
10:45 pm	Break
11:15 pm	Night Prayer: Guided Imagery (p. 97)
12:00 am	Bedtime

Saturday

8:30 am	Wake Up
9:00 am	Breakfast
9:30 am	More Community-Building (p. 72)
10:00 am	Morning Prayer (p. 101)
10:15 am	Journal Reflection and Mask-Decorating (p. 103)
11:30 am	Free Time
12:30 pm	Lunch
1:30 pm	Panel or Fishbowl Discussion on Confirmation (p. 76)
2:30 pm	Small Groups: Grace—The Gift of the Spirit (p. 105)
3:30 pm	Break/Pack Personal Belongings
4:00 pm	Prayer Service (p. 106)
5:00 pm	Retreat Ends

PART TWO: Retreats for Confirmation

Retreat Activities

Who We Are *(for both Junior-High and High-School Retreats)*

To **lead the activity:**

Divide participants into small groups prior to the retreat. Small-group leaders invite their group members to introduce themselves by sharing their names and two or three of the following:

- school
- favorite TV show, movie or song
- number of people in family
- favorite sport or activity
- an adjective which describes him- or herself.

Keep these introductions brief and on track, avoiding, at this point, the sharing of life stories. Let leaders go first to model the introductions.

Hopes and Expectations *(for both Junior-High and High-School Retreats)*

To **prepare the activity:**

Gather materials:

- newsprint, 1-2 sheets per small group
- colored felt markers, 2-3 per small group
- masking tape

To **lead the activity:**

Distribute newsprint, markers and tape to the small-group leaders. Share these guidelines for brainstorming:

- everyone participates
- whatever is said is written on the paper
- no answer is a wrong answer
- no debating

Each small-group leader places their newsprint in center of their small-group circle and asks two or three volunteers to serve as the group's "recorders," using the newsprint and markers to record the group's thoughts. At the top of one sheet of newsprint, a recorder writes: *This retreat will be disastrous if...* The group spends five minutes brainstorming all the things that would contribute to making the retreat an awful experience.

After five minutes, a recorder writes at the top of the second sheet of newsprint: *This retreat will be spectacular if...* The group brainstorms completions to this second statement for another five minutes.

Optional:
If time permits, ask small-group members to share with their groups one hope or goal that they each have for the retreat, for example:
• meet new people
• get away from pressures
• draw closer to God

This is also a good time for small-group leaders to encourage group members to support one another throughout the retreat.

Small-Group Reports *(for Junior-High and High-School Retreats)*
To **lead the activity:**
Regather the large group and invite representatives from the small groups to present the results of their brainstorming to the larger group. Team members can assist by taping the small-group lists to the walls of the meeting room.

After the final list is presented, the facilitator addressees the group with questions similar to the following:
• Which items on the "disastrous" list can we control as individuals? as a community?
• Which items on the "disastrous" list are clearly beyond our individual or collective control? *(weather, illness, acts of God, etc.)*
• Which items on the "spectacular" list can we control as individuals? as a community?
• Which items on the "spectacular" list are clearly beyond our individual or collective control?

Encourage the group to respect one another, avoid disaster and move toward the spectacular throughout the retreat.

"I Am..." *(for Junior High Retreat only)*
To **prepare the activity:**
Gather materials:
• paper
• pens or pencils

To **lead the activity:**
Divide participants into small groups. Distribute paper and pens or pencils.

Ask each candidate to write his or her name on one side of a piece of paper, then, on the other side of the paper, to write the words "I Am..." in large letters.

Share with candidates some of the "I am" statements from the Gospel of John that describe Jesus, for example:
• I am the bread of life.
• I am the good shepherd.
• I am the light of the world.
• I am the way, the truth and the life.

Explain that other people get to know us—and we can get to know ourselves better—by simply finishing our own "I am..." statements. Give candidates five to seven minutes to brainstorm as many personal completions to the "I am..." statement as they can. Encourage them to fill the paper with words describing who they are, for example:
• I am...a sister (brother).
• I am...an aunt (uncle).
• I am...an only child.
• I am...a soccer player.
• I am...afraid.
• I am...a lot of fun.
• I am...an artist.

After five to seven minutes, invite group members to read their statements to the other members of their small groups.

When all have had an opportunity to share, invite them to look back at their paper and to circle:
• the statement that means the most to them
• the statement that means the least to them
• the statement they find most surprising

If time permits, invite them also to share these reflections with their small groups.

The Story of Creation/The Story of the Candidate (for both Junior-High and High-School Retreats)

To **prepare the activity:**

Gather materials:

- blank, 8½" x 11" paper, 7 sheets per participant
- stapler or yarn
- pens or pencils, 1 per participant
- background music: tape player and instrumental tapes or CD player and instrumental CDs

Assemble journals, 1 per participant:

- Fold a stack of seven sheets of paper in half, forming a 5½" x 8½" booklet.
- Staple the fold of the booklet or tie it together with yarn.
- If desired, you could include in the journals one or more quotes from contemporaries, mystics, saints or scripture.
- If someone on the retreat team has a talent for drawing, enhance the journals with artwork.
- If you do add drawings or quotes to the journals, remember to leave plenty of blank space in which participants can write or draw their reflections.

To **lead the activity:**

Distribute pens or pencils and journals. Ask participants to write their names on the outside cover of their journals.

Explain:

- No one will read your journals during the retreat, unless you invite them to. Your journal is a sacred space meant just for you; please respect the privacy of others.
- In this activity, you will be asked to share parts of your journal with a partner of your choosing.
- Listen as I read aloud a version of Genesis 1:1-31, the story of creation.

Read aloud Genesis 1:1-31.

After the reading, continue:

- In this activity, you're invited to focus on your *own* story—the unfolding of God's unique creation in *you*.

- To begin, open your journal to the very center. Draw a timeline across the two pages, marking the following times in your life: birth, age five, age eight, age ten, age thirteen, age fifteen, age eighteen.
- As I ask each of the following questions, draw a word, phrase, symbol or picture near the age in your life during which the events took place:
  — When were you born?
  — What is your earliest memory?
  — What is one of your happiest memories, a time when you had the most fun?
  — What is one significant event that occurred in your family?
  — What is one of your saddest memories, a time that was most difficult?
  — Write the names of three people who have been or are now influential in your life.
  — Draw a symbol of your earliest image of God.
  — Draw a symbol of your current image of God.

Invite participants to share this timeline with a partner of their choosing. Remind them that they only have to share what they feel comfortable sharing.

Encourage participants to add to their timelines if additional images or memories surface during the retreat.

Made in the Image and Likeness — Masks *(for both Junior-High and High-School Retreats)*

To **prepare the activity:**

Gather Materials:
- old newspaper
- scissors or paper cutter
- several rolls of fast-setting plaster bandage material (2" x 3 yd.), 1 per every two candidates, plus 2 or 3 extras
- paper lunch bags
- 3-4 teaspoons
- petroleum jelly
- small paper cups
- facial tissues

- paper towels
- small salad bowls
- bandannas
- bowls
- 3-4 pitchers of warm water
- 3-4 buckets
- 3-4 colored felt markers
- blank, white 8½" x 14" paper
- skin care lotion
- background music: tape player and instrumental tapes or CD player and instrumental CDs

In this activity, candidates work in pairs; set up one work station for every two participants. Place stations about four feet apart, on the floor, scattered around the perimeter of the room.

Using scissors or a paper cutter, cut each roll of plaster bandage material into 1" x 3" strips. Put one roll of strips into a separate paper lunch bag, each roll thus yielding two masks. Cut up two or three extra rolls and set aside, in case extra strips are needed.

At each station place:
- 4 layers of newspaper, 2 pages wide
- 1 paper bag containing plaster bandage material
- 2 teaspoons of petroleum jelly in a small paper cup
- 2 facial tissues
- 2 paper towels
- 1 bowl
- 1 bandanna

Select instrumental music and put it in the tape or CD player.

The team member who will introduce the activity prepares a brief personal story related to trust, our uniqueness, our self-identity or partnership.

To **lead the activity:**
Introduce the activity by gathering candidates in the room that has been pre-set by the team. Briefly explain the following:
- What we will do next illustrates many themes important in the

process of confirmation: our ability to trust...in God, ourselves and others; the way in which each one of us is a unique creation of God; who we are; and the importance of partnership.

- *(Team member shares a personal story relating to one of the themes suggested above.)*
- Listen to this story from scripture: *(Leader reads Gen. 26-31, Isa. 43:1-7 or Ps. 139:13-18).*

To begin, invite participants to pair off, then to gather around one of the stations and to watch as the leader explains and demonstrates each of the mask-making steps:

1 Mask-maker helps partner use bandanna or hair tie to pull hair back away from face.
2 Mask-maker applies a thin layer of petroleum jelly to partner's entire face, especially around the hair line and just below the jaw line. (The petroleum jelly prevents the plaster material from sticking to the skin. Use extra petroleum jelly for beards, sideburns and mustaches.)
3 Partner lies back with head on newspaper.
4 Mask-maker places a thin, two-ply layer of facial tissue over partner's eyes, eyebrows, mouth and facial hair. (This is for extra protection; do not make too thick. If thicker than two layers, the plaster material will not take the form of the person's features.)
5 Mask-maker hands a paper towel to partner in case water drips down the neck or in the ears.
6 Mask-maker dips a strip of plaster bandage material into warm water, smooths the strip, and applies it on one side of partner's forehead. Mask-maker continues to apply wet strips, moving side to side, overlapping strips just a bit and smoothing out holes in the plaster as he or she goes along. *Do not try to fit the pieces together like a jigsaw puzzle. Do not move around the perimeter of the face, ending at the nose — the mask will dry quickly and fall apart. It is important to build strips from side to side from top to bottom of the face.*
7 Mask-maker puts a double layer of material around the edges of the face to strengthen the mask. *Do not put a double layer on the entire face or the person's features will not show through.*
8 Mask-maker covers the eyes and mouth as well. *Do not cover the nostrils; give the partner room to breathe.* Do, however, place a folded strip *between* the nostrils and overlap with surrounding strips. *Do*

not save the eyes, nose and mouth until the end — the other plaster will be dry and these parts will fall off the mask!

9 Bring the mask down to the jaw line but do not go under it. Leave about 1/2" of space between the edge of the mask and the beginning of the hair line. Avoid getting plaster in the partner's hair.

10 Mask-maker and partner wait 5-10 minutes for the mask to dry. In silence (the mask will not dry if the partner talks), the mask-maker helps partner to feet and takes partner on a brief walk. Mask-makers remain attentive to partner's safety, remembering that partner cannot see steps, walls, doors, etc. Mask-maker encourages partner to tune into senses: hearing, smell and touch.

11 Once the mask has "set," it may feel as if it is falling off. Mask-maker and partner find a team member for help in removing the mask.

12 Once partner removes mask, partner washes face and applies skin-care lotion.

13 Mask-maker uses marker to write partner's name on piece of paper. Mask-maker then gently lays mask on the paper to continue drying. Mask-maker returns to station and prepares to have mask made by partner.

Directions to the retreat team:
- As the leader demonstrates the activity, start the background music and encourage candidates not to talk during the activity. Stress that the mask cannot take shape if the partner talks or laughs. Establish this quiet atmosphere from the start.
- While participants perform steps 1-4 above, fill bowls with warm to hot water (not boiling)
- Assist candidates throughout the activity, encouraging mask makers.
- Periodically check water temperature in the bowls; it will be necessary to empty the bowls into buckets 2-3 times during the activity, and to refill the bowls with warm water. (Cold water will interfere with the setting of the plaster.)
- When assisting with mask removal (step 11), encourage the partner wearing the mask to move mouth, eyebrows and other facial muscles to help loosen the mask. Gently loosen the edge with the fingers.
- While some members are assisting with mask removal (step 11),

others can replenish supplies at stations to make sure there is enough plaster, warm water, etc. for the second mask.

To **debrief the activity:**
Help candidates process their mask-making experience by reflecting on several or all of the following questions, either verbally or in their journals:
- How did you feel as your mask was being made?
- How did it feel to be a mask-maker?
- Describe the experience of walking in darkness. When in your life have you felt as if you were "walking in darkness"?
- Describe the experience of leading someone who could not see.
- What did this activity say to us about risk? about trust? In what circumstances of life are you called to risk and trust?
- What does this activity say to you about your relationship with God?
- Take a look at your mask:
  — What do you notice?
  — To what degree do you recognize yourself?
- Try on someone else's mask:
  — How does it feel on your face?
  — To what degree does another person's mask fit you?
- When do you put on "masks" to fit in with others?
  — What do these "masks" look like?
  — To what degree do these masks reflect your true self?
  — How comfortable are you with these masks?
- If we mixed our masks together in a pile, how would you pick out your mask? What is one thing unique to your mask?

Night Prayer *(for both Junior-High and High-School Retreats)*
Note: The Night Prayer is a guided-imagery prayer, a form of prayer that engages the imagination and leads to personal and spiritual insights. It is also, typically, a very relaxing experience, and thus an excellent way to unwind at the end of a busy retreat day. (See the Bibliography, p. 111, for additional guided-imagery resources.)

To **prepare the prayer:**
Gather materials:
- candle
- matches

- tape player and instrumental music tape or CD Player and instrumental CD
- journals
- pens or pencils

Become familiar with the text of the guided imagery. Select soothing, instrumental background music and make sure it is ready in the tape or CD player. Place a candle in the center or front of the room. Dim the lights but do not totally darken the room.

To **lead the prayer:**
Invite participants to sit or lie on their backs in a comfortable position. Encourage them to "have their own space" away from those with whom they might be tempted to talk. Once they begin to settle, turn on the instrumental music, making sure it is loud enough to be heard but soft enough not to overpower the leader's voice. Begin the guided imagery text:

Introduction:
- During this prayer, I will be leading you through a "guided imagery." This might be a new way for some of you to pray. There is not a right way or a wrong way to pray this prayer. All you need to do is close your eyes, relax, listen to my voice and the music, pay attention to the images that come to you and allow God to speak to your heart.
- No two people in this room will have the same prayer experience because no two of you share the same imagination. Pay attention to the uniqueness and the gift of your experience.

Relaxation:
- Begin by taking a deep breath. Inhale and then exhale. Take another breath, filling your lungs fully, then emptying them with a sigh. One more time, take a deep breath in, breathing in the breath of the Spirit, and then exhale, breathing out worry, fear and anxiety.
- Now think about relaxing your body, from head to toe. First, focus your attention on your feet, tightening the muscles; hold the tension, then release. Repeat this another time with your feet: tighten...hold...release.
- Now concentrate on your calves: tighten the muscles...hold...then release.

- Now tighten the muscles of your thighs: hold it...now release. Do that one more time.
- Now tighten the muscles in your hips: hold for a few seconds...then release. Repeat.
- Focus on the muscles in your abdomen: tighten...hold...release. Repeat.
- Now move to your chest and shoulders: tighten...hold...release. Repeat.
- Tighten the muscles in your hands and arms: hold...release. Repeat.
- Finally, tighten the muscles in your face: hold them...now release. Repeat.
- Now scan your own body and notice any areas of tension. Tighten those areas where you still note tension...hold them...and release.
- Continue to be aware of your breath moving in and out of your lungs. Breath in life and peace and let go of worry and anxiety.

Guided Imagery:
- I am going to guide you on an imaginary journey. Pay attention to the images that come to you. Begin by imagining that you are walking along a winding river. Look around you as you walk. What colors do you see? What sounds do you hear? What do you smell? *(Pause.)*
- Continue walking, feeling the firmness of the earth beneath you supporting you on your journey. Notice the water in the river—its color...its flow...its sound. *(Pause.)*
- As you walk, you hear someone gently calling your name. You follow the sounds of the voice until you see a person sitting on a log next to a small fire. Somehow, instinctively, you know you can trust this person. As you move closer, notice what the person is wearing. What does this person's face look like? *(Pause.)*
- You sit down and begin to listen to what the person has to say. The person tells you that you have been made in the image and likeness of God. You are a unique part of God's creation. God formed you within your mother's womb. God loves you more than you can imagine. Now it is your turn to speak. What is it that you want to say to this person? Spend a few moments talking and listening. *(Pause.)*
- The person tells you that the time has come for you to leave. As the two of you stand up, the person takes a small object from a pocket and places it in your hand. The object is a reminder of your conver-

sation. After saying goodbye, you turn and walk back along the river. As you carry the object with you, notice how you are feeling after your encounter with this person. *(Pause.)*

Conclusion:
- Slowly, quietly, begin to focus again on the sounds in this room...the sound of my voice...the sound of the music...the sounds of the people around you.
- Open your eyes, and when you feel ready, slowly sit up and stretch.
- If you notice that someone around you has fallen asleep, gently wake them up.

Distribute pens or pencils and participants' journals. Say:
- I mentioned at the beginning of this prayer experience that, although we were "praying in a group," no two people in the room would have the same prayer experience.
- Before we talk about this experience, I would like you to take a few minutes and write in your journal about it. Perhaps you want to describe the person you met along the river or the small object that was presented to you. You might even want to record some of your conversation with the person.

After a few minutes, gather the group for a discussion. Because guided imagery can be a very personal prayer experience, explain that there is no pressure to share. Ask a few open-ended questions to get the discussion going, for example:
- What happened in your prayer?
- What did you notice?
- How did you feel?

Note: Guided imagery sometimes elicits uncomfortable feelings or memories. Be attentive to the body language of participants. Encourage anyone who seems to be struggling to talk with one of the team members afterwards.

Morning Prayer *(for both Junior-High and High-School Retreats)*
To **prepare the prayer:**
Gather materials:
- table
- small stones, 1 per participant

- freezer
- Bible
- 2 large clear bowls
- 2 pitchers of water
- 2 hand towels
- tape player and instrumental music tape or CD Player and instrumental CD
- songbooks or songsheets, 1 per participant

Place the stones in the freezer at least eight hours before the prayer. Take the stones out of the freezer just before beginning the prayer.

Place the empty bowls, pitchers of water and hand towels on a small table in the center of the room. Open the Bible to Ezekiel 36:24-28.

From the songbooks or songsheets choose one or two songs or short refrains that focus on the themes of morning, water, creation or new life.

Put the tape or CD in the tape or CD player so it is ready when the prayer begins.

To **lead the prayer:**
(Presider gathers the group in a circle around the table with the pitchers of water, large bowls and towels.)

Opening Song

Opening Prayer

> *Presider:*
> God of all creation, we gather this morning to welcome this new day, your gift to us. We know that you created each of us in your image and likeness. You formed us in the secret of our mothers' wombs. You call each of us by name to walk with you this day. Bless us as we begin this second day of our retreat. May our hearts be open to all that you have to teach us today. We pray this prayer in the name of Jesus, our brother.

> *All:*
> Amen.

(Presider invites all to be seated. As team members place one frozen stone in front of each participant. Presider asks participants to look at the stones but not to touch them.)

Scripture Reading: Ezekiel 36:24-28

Presider:
I now invite you to pick up the stone in front of you. As you hold the stone, what do you notice about it? Close your eyes and listen again to these words of the prophet Ezekiel:

> I will give you a new heart and place a new spirit within you, taking from your bodies your stony hearts and giving you [hearts of flesh] (Ezek. 36:26).

What part of your heart is like this cold, hard stone? What part of your heart needs to be removed? Think for a moment about one way that you would like to change your own heart? *(Pause.)*

Now focus again on the stone in your hand. Does it feel different than it did when you first began to hold it? Has the temperature of the stone changed? How might God be able to help you change your cold stony heart to a natural heart? *(Pause.)*

Open your eyes and bring your attention to the center of the room. In just a moment, I will invite each of you to come forward, when you are ready, to one of the bowls. Place your stone in the bowl as a sign of your willingness to change your heart. Then, place your hands over the bowl, and one of the team members will pour water over your hands and repeat the words of Ezekiel: "I will sprinkle clean water upon you to cleanse you..." (Ezek. 36:25a). You may dry your hands with a towel if you like, and then return to your seat.

Please focus you attention on the people in the center of the room and silently pray for them.

(Turn on instrumental music or begin singing a simple refrain. When all who wish to come to the center have done so, continue the prayer:)

Presider:
Let us stand and pray the prayer that Jesus taught us:

Lord's Prayer

Presider:
Jesus came to bring us peace. As we end our prayer this morning, let us turn to one another and offer a sign of that peace.

Sign of Peace

Journal Reflection and Mask Decorating *(for both Junior-High and High-School Retreats)*
To **prepare the activity:**
Gather materials:
- journals
- pens or pencils
- masks created earlier in the retreat
- art supplies: poster paints, brushes, colored tissue paper, glitter, feathers, foil, pipe cleaners, markers, glue, scissors etc.
- tape player and instrumental music tape or CD Player and instrumental CD
- brooms or vacuum cleaner
- garbage bags

Spread the art supplies on several tables. Set up the CD or tape player.

To **lead the activity:**
Ask each candidate to take his or her mask, journal and a pen or pencil and to find a place in the room where they can have some privacy. Explain that you are going to lead the group through a journaling exercise which focuses on "rites of passage." Discuss:
- What does the term *rite of passage* mean? *(significant moments or turning points in a person's life)*
- What examples of rites of passage can we think of? *(birth, baptism, marriage, divorce, graduation, a new understanding, an injury, etc.)*

Explain:

- During this exercise, think of significant events or periods in your lives when you moved from one way of being to a new way of being or understanding.
- To start, on a blank page in your journal, write one or two rites of passage that occurred during your life between birth and two years old. You do not necessarily have to remember these; just note that they happened. *(Offer these examples, if necessary: birth, baptism, learning to walk, learning to talk, divorce or death in family, moving to a new home.)*
- Now think of the time between the ages of three and six. Write one or two rites of passage that occurred during this time. *(Offer examples: going to school, losing a tooth, beginning to play a sport, learning to ride a bike, beginning to study one of the arts, a significant event in family life.)*
- Focus now on the time between the ages of seven and ten. Name one or two rites of passage from this period. *(Offer, examples: first communion, first reconciliation, change in family life, change in school, change in friends.)*
- Reflect now on your life from the time you were eleven until the age of fourteen. Write two significant rites of passage that took place during this time. *(Offer, examples: moving from one grade to another, puberty, dating, change in family life.)*
- *(For High-School Retreats:)* Look now at the time between age fifteen and the present. Name two rites of passage that have occurred during this recent time period. *(Offer examples: dating, driving, getting a job, change in family life, change in school.)*
- Now write down one rite of passage from this retreat, when you moved from one way of thinking or being to another. *(Offer examples: meeting new people, mask-making, trust walk, Hearts of Stone ritual.)*
- Finally, think about your relationship with God. Write down a significant event or time which changed your relationship with God, for better or for worse.
- Look back over these new journal entries and select one rite of passage from each age category. You should have seven rites of passage.
- Using the art materials provided, continue to reflect on those rites of passage by symbolizing them on your mask. The symbols need not correspond to the actual feature on the mask, although some-

times that is appropriate; for example, for a sad event, someone might paint a tear by an eye. If you need help thinking of ideas, ask a member of the retreat team.

As candidates work, give them a fifteen-, a five- and a two-minute warning. Throughout the time, encourage them to continue moving through the activity. If they get stuck on how to symbolize something, ask them to move on and come back to it.

When time is called, use the garbage bags and brooms or the vacuum cleaner to clean up the area.

Participants then return to their small groups to reflect on their activity; give volunteers a chance to talk about any parts of their masks. Make certain each member has an opportunity to talk. Watch the time and keep the group on track; once candidates begin to share stories, the time can disappear quickly!

(For High-School Retreats:)
In small groups, continue the discussion:
• What cultural celebrations or ceremonies that mark our rites of passage?
• What are the Church's sacraments of initiation?
• How are the sacraments of initiation celebrations of our rites of passage?

Grace — Gift of the Spirit *(for both Junior-High and High-School Retreats)*
To **prepare the activity:**
Gather materials:
• scissors, 1 per small group
• 8" pieces of ribbon or yarn, 7 per participant
• 1" x 4" strips of colored construction paper, 7 per participant
• pens or pencils, 1 per participant
• masks created earlier in the retreat

To **lead the activity:**
Return to the small groups. Small-group leader asks participants to name some of the gifts of the Spirit. Discuss examples of how they currently see these gifts in their own lives or in the lives of others.

After several minutes of discussion, leaders distribute pens or pencils, ribbon and construction-paper strips. Invite group members to think of seven areas in their lives in which they would like the grace of God's Spirit. In other words, if they could ask God to help them with seven things, what would these be? As they think of these areas, ask them to write each one on a separate slip of construction paper. After writing their seven ideas, they fold each slip three or four times.

The small-group leader then passes the scissors around the group and asks each candidate to poke seven holes in their mask and one hole in each of their pieces of construction paper.

Participants then tie one end of each of their pieces of ribbon or yarn through the holes on the mask. They tie the other end of each piece of ribbon or yarn to a separate slip of their construction paper.

If time permits, ask each small group to form a circle and close with this silent prayer: One at a time, invite each member to stand in the center of the circle with his or her mask. Other members each place a hand on the shoulder, head, back or arm of the person and pray silently for him or her.

Prayer Service *(for both Junior-High and High-School Retreats)*
To **prepare the service:**
Gather materials:
- 1 large candle
- small taper candles with wax guards, 1 per participant
- basket
- matches
- small table
- masks created earlier in the retreat

In the center of the group circle, on the small table, place the large candle and matches. Put the wax guards on the small tapers and place them in a basket beside the table. Arrange the candidates' masks on the floor on the outside of the circle.

Select a simple refrain or song focusing on the themes of sending forth, being light in the world or commissioning. Because participants will already be holding masks and candles, use a familiar refrain so they will not need songsheets.

To **lead the service:**
(Invite participants to enter the room; ask them to find and sit in front of their own masks, facing the center of the circle.)

Opening Song

Opening Prayer

> *Presider:*
> Let us begin our prayer in the name of the Father and of the Son and of the Holy Spirit.

> *All:*
> Amen.

> *Presider:*
> *(Light large candle and say:)* Good and gracious God, we come together at the end of this retreat to give you thanks for the gifts that you have showered upon us. We are your servants, your chosen, the ones you have called by name. We pray that you will send your Spirit to us so that we might continue to walk forward in faith to proclaim your goodness to the world. We ask this in the name of Jesus, our brother.

> *All:*
> Amen.

Scripture: Matthew 5:13-16

> *Presider:*
> Let us take just a few minutes to reflect on how we are salt of the earth and light for the world.

> *(Observe a brief period of silence.)*

> *Presider:*
> We are each called to be salt for the earth and light for the world. God calls us to take what we have learned here and share it with

others. As we begin to draw our retreat to a close, I invite you to think of two things: First, what one new insight or thought have you gained through this retreat *(If necessary, share examples: I learned that I am unique; I deepened my relationship with God; I met new friends; I learned that I can trust others or myself.)* Second, as you think about moving forward from this experience, what do you need from God, this community or the larger Christian community in order to grow in faith? *(Again, if necessary, share examples: courage, encouragement, acceptance, hugs.)* Take a few minutes to think about what you have gained from this experience and what you will continue to seek.

(Observe another brief period of silence.)

Presider:
In just a moment, a team member will call each of you by name to come into the center of the circle. *(Example: "John, I call you by name.")* When you come forward, claim your mask, put it on and slowly turn around so that the entire group can see an image of God and the symbols of your rites of passage. Then, one of the team members will ask you two questions:
• What have you learned on your faith journey this weekend?
• What do you ask of God and this community?

After you have spoken, a team member will light a candle and present it to you saying, "Go forth and be light for the world." You may take your candle and return to your place in the circle.

(Retreat team begins calling candidates by name, one at a time, in any order, asking the questions and presenting the candles. When all have finished, presider continues the prayer:)

Presider:
Let us stand and pray. Jesus taught us that prayer is an important part of any faith journey. Let us pray together the prayer that Jesus taught us:

Lord's Prayer

Presider:

The candles we hold are symbols of the light of Christ that burns within each of us. God promises to warm our hearts by removing our hearts of stone and giving us hearts of flesh. I invite you to extinguish your candle, knowing that the light is within you. Before we depart from this place, I invite you to offer one another a sign of Christ's peace.

Sign of Peace

Closing Song

Bibliography

Liturgical Resources

Connel, Martin, ed. *The Catechetical Documents: A Parish Resource.* Chicago: Liturgy Training Publications, 1996.

Hoffman, Elizabeth, ed. *The Liturgy Documents: A Parish Resource,* 3rd edition. Chicago: Liturgy Training Publications, 1991.

Lectionary for Mass. New York: Catholic Book Publishing Company, 1974.

Lectionary for Masses with Children, Volumes A, B and C. Collegeville, Minn.: The Liturgical Press, 1993, 1994.

The Rites of the Catholic Church, Volume One. Collegeville, Minn.: The Liturgical Press, 1990.

The Sacramentary. New York: Catholic Book Publishing Company, 1985.

Tufano, Victoria, ed. *Sourcebook for Sundays and Seasons.* Chicago: Liturgy Training Publications, annual.

Music Resources

Gather Comprehensive. Chicago: GIA Publications, 1994.

Journeysongs. Portland, Oregon: Ore.: Oregon Catholic Press, 1994.

Ritual Song: A Hymnal and Service Book for Roman Catholics. Chicago: GIA Publications, 1996.

Worship: A Hymnal and Service Book for Roman Catholics. Chicago: GIA Publications, 1986.

Community Building and Icebreaker Resources

Chesto, Kathleen. *Rituals and Icebreakers — Practical Tools for Forming Community.* Kansas City, Mo.: Sheed and Ward, 1995.

Fluegelman, Andrew. *New Games* and *More New Games.* New York, N.Y.: Doubleday, 1981.

Rice and Yaconelli. *Play It!* El Cajon, Cal.: Youth Specialities, 1986.

Rohnke, Karl. *Silver Bullets — A Guide to Initiative Problems, Adventure Games and Trust Activities*. Hamilton, Mass.: Project Adventure, 1984.

Weinstein, Matt and Joel Goodman. *Playfair*, San Luis Obispo, Cal.: Impact Publications, 1988.

Guided Imagery Resources

Arsenault, Jane E. and Jean R. Cedor. *Guided Meditations for Youth on Sacramental Life*. Winona, Minn.: St. Mary's Press, 1993.

Murdock, Maureen. *Spinning Inward, Using Guided Imagery with Children for Learning* and *Creativity and Relaxation*. Boston, Mass.: Shambala Publications, Inc. 1987.

Prayer and Retreat Resources

Dockrey, Karen. *Junior High Retreats and Lock-Ins*. Loveland, Colo.: Group Books, 1990.

Froehle, Virginia Ann, R.S.M. *Called Into Her Presence*. Notre Dame, In.: Ave Maria Press, 1992.

Grgic, Bob. *Resources for Outdoor Retreats*. Winona, Minn.: St. Mary's Press. 1994.

Haas, David. *Psalm Prayers*. Cincinnati, O.: St. Anthony Messenger Press, 1994.

Hakowski, Maryann. *Pathways to Praying with Teens*. Winona, Minn.: Saint Mary's Press, 1993.

————. *PrayerWays: Teaching Manual*. Winona, Minn.: St. Mary's Press, 1995.

————. *Vine and Branches, Vol. 1, Resources for Youth Retreats*. Winona, Minn.: St. Mary's Press, 1992.

————. *Vine and Branches, Vol. 2, Resources for Youth Retreats*. Winona, Minn.: St. Mary's Press, 1992.

————. *Vine and Branches, Vol. 3, Resources for Youth Retreats.* Winona, Minn.: St. Mary's Press, 1994.

Koch, Carl, FSC. *PrayerWays.* Winona, Minn.: St. Mary's Press, 1995.

Lanciotti, Judi. *Prayers with Pizzazz for Junior High Teens.* Winona, Minn.: St. Mary's Press, 1996.

The Liturgical Documents, A Parish Resource, Third Edition. Chicago, Ill.: Liturgy Training Publications, 1991.